OUR OWN MATILDA

BARBARA WALL developed an interest in the novels of early South Australian author 'Maud Jeanne Franc' when she came upon them while researching South Australian children's fiction. She had formerly written on children's literature in *The Narrator's Voice: The Dilemma of Children's Fiction* (Macmillan, 1991).

Her thirty years as a teacher of English in South Australian schools has provided a foundation for this study of the work of a writer who was herself a teacher.

Our Own Matilda

Matilda Jane Evans
1827–1886

Pioneer Woman and Novelist

Barbara Wall

Wakefield Press

Wakefield Press
Box 2266
Kent Town
South Australia 5071

First published 1994

Cover design by Kerry Argent
Book design and typesetting by Michael Deves
Printed and bound by Hyde Park Press, Adelaide

National Library of Australia
Cataloguing-in-publication entry

Wall, Barbara, 1926-
Our Own Matilda.
Bibliography.
Includes index.

ISBN 1 86254 329 1.

1. Franc, Maud Jeanne, 1827-1886. 2. Franc, Maud Jeanne, 1827-1886 -
Bibliography. 3. Congreve, H.J. (Henry John), 1829-1918. 4. Congreve,
H.J. (Henry John), 1829-1918 - Bibliography. 5. Austhors, Australian -
19th century - Biography. 6. Authors, Australian - South Australia -
Biography. 7. Women authors - Australia - Biography. 8. Women
pioneers - Australia - Biography. I. Title.

A823.1

To Mary and the girls

Author's note

Many people have helped me. Librarians of Special Collections in libraries all over Australia generously answered my letters and provided the information on which the bibliography is based. The staff of the State Library of South Australia have been consistently helpful. I am particularly grateful to Valmai Hankel, Elizabeth Ho, Juliana Bayfield and Valerie Sitters, and to all the staff of the Mortlock Library.

Margaret Allen gave me access to the material she had collected on Matilda Evans and stimulated me to delve deeper. Marjorie Roe did essential research in Queensland and Julie Evans, in the course of her own research, has kept an eye open for Congreve, Evans and Franc. Douglas Muecke has been encumbered with with research requests every time he has left for Sydney or Melbourne for the last four years. He has been indefatigable and meticulous, and has in addition read drafts, located errors and made helpful suggestions. I am deeply grateful to these four people.

Special thanks go to John Congreve of Sydney, great-great nephew of Matilda Evans, for allowing me to see the Congreve papers, and for permission to quote from Matilda's letters. I also thank Michael Bollen and the Wakefield Press, Paul and Monica Depasquale, Sue and Newton Lines, Marcie Muir and Beryl Linn and the members of the Tatlers' Club. I have been helped and encouraged by the support of the Women's Suffrage Centenary Steering Committee, and am especially grateful for the assistance of Jean Blackburn and Muriel Ellis.

Mary Teesdale Smith explored the countryside with me as I tried to find the places where Matilda and her husband had lived and worked, and shared my pleasure in the discoveries. Her interest and support have been invaluable.

Contents

Matilda Jane Evans

Preface

The Colony of South Australia was not much more than twenty-two years old when, on Wednesday, 25 May 1859, the following advertisement appeared on the front page of *The South Australian Register*, Adelaide's leading daily paper.

Will be published on the 1st June next, Part I of
M ARIAN, or THE LIGHT OF SOME ONE'S HOME; A Tale of Australian Life in the Bush. By Maud Jean Franc.
This work will be issued in monthly numbers, price 1s.6d. each, and when complete will form a very handsome volume in elegantly gilt cloth. The publishers pledge themselves to spare no trouble in making this work superior in style to any that has yet emanated from the colonial press.
Mount Barker: Alfred Waddy. Adelaide: W.H. Hillier, and all Booksellers.

It was a daring undertaking, testifying to the faith of the publisher and the author in the enterprise. The four parts of what was to prove Franc's most popular novel, four elegant little volumes with pretty, decorated, pastel paper covers, appeared between June and September 1859, and were well received in the colony. Nothing like this—the publishing of a novel in parts—had been done before in South Australia, nor had the colony been so cheerfully and pleasantly celebrated. Here was a story by a South Australian for South Australians. And if it was moral and simple and religious and uneventful, that is what ambitious colonists wanted for their wives and daughters, and they were certainly not

1

averse to reading it themselves. It was a novelty, and a worthwhile novelty. The first part sold out quickly. When the *Victorian Monthly Magazine* reviewed the first part in July, barely a month after its first appearance, the reviewer was looking at the second edition. By the end of the year the parts were being bound together. The Mortlock Library in South Australia has a copy of this first edition, with a preface by 'the Authoress, Mount Barker, September, 1859'.

The authoress, as she usually styled herself, was at that time thirty-two years of age. Her name was Matilda Congreve and she kept a school in Mount Barker. She had come from England and had been in South Australia for seven years. *Marian* was the first of fourteen novels and many stories, all of which have something to tell us about the way ordinary middle-class people adapted to life in the colony.

Marian was not the first novel by a South Australian. *Clara Morison: A Tale of South Australia during the Gold Fever* by Catherine Helen Spence had appeared in 1854, and *Tender and True: A Colonial Tale* in 1856. But they were published in England and were not readily available in South Australia. *Clara Morison* was not reviewed here at all and when *Tender and True* was reviewed in *The Adelaide Observer*, the writer pointed out that it was 'not to be purchased in Adelaide'. An article in the *Australian Family Herald* in August 1877 noted that Spence's novels were published at such a high price that they could never be popular in South Australia.

Nor was *Marian* the first novel to be published in South Australia. *The Queen of the South: A Colonial Romance. Being Pictures of life in Victoria in the Early Days of the Diggings* by 'A. Pendragon' [George Isaacs] had been published by W. Barnet at Gawler in 1858. Not much is known about its success—it was set entirely in Victoria, and it was not reprinted.

But *Marian* was certainly the first novel by a woman to be published in South Australia, and the first novel to be wholly set in South Australia. Its manner of publication—in parts, at 1s. 6d. each—made it possible for many different kinds of people to try this new local work. That they did try it, and liked it, is proved by the immediate need for a second edition. Reviews can be found in most of the papers which survive from this time, reviews which express pride in the achievement of a local writer, as well as wonder that the publication had happened at all. The novel was felt to be a story remarkable for its truth to life. It was praised for the purity of its tone, for 'the exquisite appreciation of external nature' shown by the author, and for 'the admirable fidelity' of its descriptive passages. While it was acknowledged that 'the very faithful picture of bush life' lacked outstanding characters and dramatic action, the reviewers appeared proud that the ordinary life of the colony had been celebrated and they were pleased rather than perturbed by the author's strong religious purpose. And though they did not say so explicitly they clearly liked the positive tone and the hopeful views given of the colony and its future, for the heroine Marian, like most of the readers of the story, had come from England, and without much in the way of resources was determined to be independent and to succeed. If she married at the end and was henceforth to be supported by a wealthy husband, it was not before she had shown herself capable of supporting herself; and her love for, and faith in, the colony had grown steadily as the story progressed.

Novels which set out deliberately, as *Marian* did, to inculcate religious principles are seldom valued today, but in their own day Matilda's novels were both popular and—in a small way—influential. This is indisputable since they were reprinted so many times; indeed six were reprinted as late as the mid-1920s, forty years after her death. The number of copies still available in antiquarian bookshops, and the three hundred or so to be found in the special collections of Australian libraries, to say nothing of those in private collections, also testify to their popularity. The novels clearly met a need in the colony.

The woman who wrote them had much in common with a large proportion of the colonists. Many, like Matilda, had arrived in South Australia, impoverished, with a fortune to make. Many, like her, were Dissenters, attracted to the colony by the views of men like George Fife Angas, Robert Gouger and Rowland Hill, who saw South Australia as a place where pious men and woman

3

might live according to God and their consciences without interference from the State. The breaking of ties with Great Britain had encouraged many immigrants to break as well their ties with the Church and with religion. Matilda showed in her writings that she saw it as her religious duty to provide stories which might bring them back to religion. Clearly she enjoyed writing, and she always needed money, but without doubt one of her chief purposes in writing, as she said in the preface to *Marian*, was 'to exhibit the beauty of true Religion as exemplified in the daily walk of life'. She hoped to provide religious teaching to those who had grown up without it, and to strengthen and sustain the faith of those for whom attendance at Church was not always possible in a colony in which there were few places of worship. Later, churches and chapels were built, but for those without carts or buggies or their own horses the long distances were discouraging. For Dissenters the truth could be found in Bible study, and they believed that from that study faith would follow. This was a lesson which might be conveyed in fiction. Matilda's characters carry their Bibles with them and study them constantly, and those who wish to believe but cannot are always directed to read the Bible until faith comes. Bible study and the conviction that it is the mission of all Christians to convert others are at the heart of all Matilda's novels.

Didactic, religious, temperance novels—for Matilda soon became known as a writer who could vividly portray the evils so often attendant upon indulgence in the 'strong colonial wine'— may not be much respected today, but Matilda herself was highly respectable, and her novels contain much to interest the student of the early days of the colony. Though they were read by men as well as women, and have male as well as female protagonists, they show life in the colony primarily from a woman's point of view. They deal with domestic crises and personal relationships, with those who succeed through hard work and those whose lives are destroyed by alcoholic brutality, with comfortably-off people as well as with those who struggle. They deal with death and with the comfort that religion can bring to the dying and to the bereaved. A glance at the mortality figures in the years during which Matilda wrote, particularly those for children, help us to see why writers like Matilda set out in their stories to help their readers cope with the trauma associated with infant death, with death from tuberculosis, and with death from alcoholism.

Because she was a woman of great grit and determination who succeeded in the face of much personal sorrow and adversity, because she gave a real—though certainly limited—picture of certain aspects of domestic and small town life, because her work proved so popular, and because she was the first woman novelist to be published in South Australia, I believe that Matilda and her stories are well worth writing about. Her world is very different from ours, yet surprisingly I have found much that is familiar to me from my own childhood and from the stories of their child-hoods told to me by my parents.

The Baptist church, its services and its strong emotional language, the strict Sunday observance, the fear of alcohol, the distrust of Anglicanism were all part of my childhood. Everyone knew about pledge books, and indeed I was persuaded by an earnest and determined young Sunday-school teacher to 'sign the pledge' myself at the age of nine or ten, in complete ignorance of what it meant. I did not live in a country town, but in the 1920s and the early days of the depression, the northern suburbs of Adelaide were not so very much different. The paddocks began two streets north of us, there were empty blocks everywhere, and we walked to the dairy each morning to watch the milking and to collect the milk still warm from the cow. The big house, in its own grounds, stood up on the hill. Matilda's world seems closer to the world of my childhood than the world of later and more cele-brated writers like Lawson and Henry Handel Richardson.

Suzanne Falkiner in *Settlement*, her recent illuminating study of writers and landscape, notes that 'country towns have not been treated kindly by Australian writers' and that 'the small, raw, developing urban settlements of Australia have suffered the same prejudices as the landscape and have been described largely in terms of what they lacked' (p. 13). Writing of South Australia she concentrated on the work of Catherine Spence, Barbara Hanrahan, Hal Porter, Nicholas Jose and Murray Bail, all writers critical of the world they live in, and several of them possessed of highly idiosyncratic viewpoints. In the work of a lesser writer—a writer who accepted her world and concerned herself not with 'the great world' but with the task of improving the behaviour of individuals, a writer without great literary gifts who set out to describe what she saw around her and the kind of people she knew, in a sense a very ordinary woman writing for ordinary readers—we do find an attractive picture of little, developing country towns, and of small centres in the suburbs of Adelaide. We can find a believable 1850s and 1860s Adelaide and believable small-town life in the pages of the novels of Maud Jeanne Franc.

Although the Dissenters who came to South Australia in the early days were in a minority, many of them were very active and enthusiastic, and made a lasting impact on South Australian society. Adelaide indeed became known as the 'city of churches', an image which its inhabitants have never been able to shake off. George Fife Angas, perhaps the most influential of all these pioneering evangelical Protestants, was a Baptist, and he certainly knew and approved of Matilda. His son, George French Angas, provided illustrations for two of the novels Matilda wrote while she was living in the Angaston area. In these novels, and in those that followed, we find a picture of an intense religious life. Today Matilda's views often seem narrow and limited, even blinkered, but I think there is no doubt that her stories reflect the religious attitudes of a devout and influential section of early South Australian society. An autobiographical account of the same stern principles at work can be found in *Colonial Life and Christian Experience* by George Fife Angas's secretary, Henry Hussey, which deals with the same period. (Hussey does not mention Matilda but his son H.B. Hussey illustrated the *South Australian Christmas Annual* of 1881 to which Matilda was a contributor.) From her books we can discover what it was like to live in such a society.

Not much is known about Matilda's life, and everything in print contains some inaccuracies. There are few family papers; apparently only three holograph letters. Newspapers, which are not always reliable, and public records have been my chief source. The novels and stories undoubtedly tell us a great deal about her life, her work and her personality, but what is fact and what is fiction—who knows? In the absence of other information, I have read what she has written, and speculated. I have lived with her novels for five years and this has certainly given me some understanding of the personality of Maud Jeanne Franc. But Matilda, too, who triumphed over so many difficulties to become respected both as an author and as a schoolmistress, has become real to me. I have very much enjoyed researching her life, reading her books and unravelling the problems connected with the many reprints of her work. She made an outstanding contribution to the culture of her time in South Australia, and neither she nor her work should be forgotten.

My study of her life will I hope add something to our understanding of the history of the early years of South Australia. The detailed and annotated 'Bibliography of the Works of Maud Jeanne Franc' with which this book concludes will make it easy for copies of her novels, so often issued undated, to be assigned to the appropriate date, will substantiate my claims that her work was popular, and will also add something to the history of printing and publishing in South Australia and London in Victorian times.

Barbara Wall, Adelaide 1994

Marian and Allen
"All this day and not a word together!"

Three different responses to the same scene – 1860, 1868 and 1920s
(Mortlock Collection)

PART ONE

Woman and Writer

The South Rhine Baptist Church was opened in 1863. It is now a hay shed.

The house in French Street, Angaston, in which Matilda conducted a boarding school.

CHAPTER I

Scattered Fortunes

Matilda Jane Congreve, well-brought-up, accomplished, and with strong religious principles, arrived in Adelaide in the early days of the colony, and those early days are the settings for most of her novels. She did not come to a comfortable existence and the first twenty years of her life in the colony must have been a struggle indeed, with much personal sorrow and anguish, and considerable hardship. Yet if we accept the constantly tranquil and accepting tone of her fictions as evidence of her attitude, we must conclude that she faced these troubles with great fortitude and firmness. Her achievements certainly suggest this.

Problems arose for her from the moment of her arrival, and indeed before. Her family were impoverished gentlefolk, and it seems likely that they came to Australia believing poverty and a working existence would be easier to bear in a faraway country. This is certainly the impression given by the narrator of *Golden Gifts*, one of Matilda's early novels, which deals with a family of young siblings emigrating in similar circumstances. At the same time Matilda's positive attitude to life and what lies ahead is suggested by the characters' dreams of the future and the emphasis on freedom.

> They must throw off the shackles of society, and put their unwonted hands to the plough, that was certain. But could they do that in England? No; a touch of old family pride declared that at once. Why not then in Australia? why not? Not a dissenting voice answered the question. For many reasons that was decidedly the land for carrying the threads of their scattered fortunes; and that night they went to bed to

> dream of the long voyage and its termination—of a long
> farewell to conventionalism, and a welcome to freedom of
> thought, and feeling, and action.
>
> *Golden Gifts*, p. 7

In her printed writings, which, with the exception of a few letters, is all we have, Matilda is always positive—she accepts what happens, always believing and trusting in God, and hopes for the best. But a comment made by her sister Emily, who was also a writer and schoolteacher, in one of the stories in her book *Colonial Pen-Scratchings*, suggests other possible attitudes: 'Ah! nobody knows the miseries of the elegant poor—the poor who have once been rich'. Emily's stories and sketches frequently make an interesting contrast with Matilda's. She is negative, where Matilda is positive. Emily's view of life is often tinged with self-pity—she seems to have had some difficulty in adapting to colonial life. Her uncertainty seems to be epitomised by her adoption of a curiously tentative male pseudonym, 'Little Jacob'. Nevertheless some of her stories are apparently based on incidents in the lives of the family and add something to our knowledge of how they saw themselves in this new world.

It seems unlikely that Matilda's earlier life could have prepared her for what she would have to face in Australia. She came from distinguished and wealthy families on both sides, and although they were Baptists and therefore not in the mainstream of society, they were professional people and leaders in their fields. Growing up with aspirations to be a writer, like so many in a family which numbered the dramatist William Congreve amongst its members, she could hardly have imagined that her early adulthood would be spent as a struggling schoolteacher in small South Australian towns. But the talent and energy which had led her to produce, at the age of fourteen, a small volume of poems for the young, for the copyright of which she received £10, enabled her to surmount one difficulty after another until she too became a professional, in the two fields of teaching and writing.

She was born on 27 August 1827 at Peckham in Surrey, the second daughter of Henry Congreve (1793-1852) and Elizabeth Ann Jacob (1804-1852), daughter of Benjamin Jacob, an eminent musician who was for many years organist of Surrey Chapel. At the time of his marriage to Elizabeth, Henry had one child, George Thomas Congreve, from a previous marriage to Lucy Hoppe (1798-1823). A daughter of that marriage, Lucy, had died as an infant. The first child of his marriage to Elizabeth, Lydia Jacob Congreve, also died as an infant, but the others, Matilda, Henry John, Emily, William, Frederick Jacob and James all emigrated to Australia. Matilda kept in touch with George and his family, who remained in England, all her life.

Henry Congreve, the father, seems to have been a man of curious instability. His own father, George Thomas Congreve of Bedworth, County Warwick, was a surgeon and apparently a wealthy man. He and his wife, Hester Watts, a relation of Isaac Watts, the hymn writer, were devout Christians and provided a strong religious upbringing for their three sons, of whom Henry was the second. Henry was apprenticed to a ribbon manufacturer of Coventry and during that time and afterwards he became very unsteady, disappointing his parents by frequenting balls and theatres and rejecting religion. By 1814 however he had experienced some kind of conversion, and with his two brothers joined the church at Bedworth. In 1824 he moved to Peckham and at about the time of his second marriage joined the Baptist Church there. He was a very active and useful member for twenty-eight years; for the last nine years he was a deacon. His son Henry John however makes it clear that though Henry's personal conduct became exemplary with his conversion to Christianity, he remained unsteady all his life where money was concerned. Dr Congreve, his father, twice presented him with £10,000, and twice he lost this money through speculations. This deeply affected his family. His daughters, Matilda and Emily, both write of the problems caused by spec-ulation in their fictions. Emily, indeed, in her story 'Little Cary's Experiences as a "New Chum"' is surely fictionalising her own family. She calls the emigrating father Harry Cleve, a name very close to Henry Congreve, and he dies soon after arrival in Adelaide in a manner resembling the way her father died. According to Emily, Harry's change of fortunes, which caused the family to emigrate, was dramatic and traumatic.

> For a time Harry Cleve, was the richest merchant in London,
> till he speculated—then a change came, demolishing the
> foundations of a fortune he was rapidly realizing; a fortune a
> thousand times surpassing the inheritance of his elder brother
> —but it all went now.
>
> *Colonial Pen-Scratchings*, p.48

At some time Henry studied medicine under his father and later became a specialist in the cure of consumption. According to his son he was very successful—which is ironic since his wife Elizabeth apparently died of consumption. He published a number of books, including *New Era in Medical Science. Consumption curable: observations on the treatment of pulmonary diseases*, and *The Nursery Gem; or the Physical and mental education and management of children, from an early age*. His son, George, who remained in England, continued his work on consumption, and published a small book *On Consumption of the Lungs, or Decline, and the only successful treatment: showing that formidable disease to be curable in all its stages*. This work had gone through twenty-three editions by 1857, and was still being republished in 1911. It was in fact published in Australia and New Zealand (in South Australia by Rigby), and was certainly available in Adelaide in 1888—as was also Congreve's 'Balsamic Elixir for Catarrh, Coughs and Colds' which was extensively advertised in local papers.

Although Henry achieved considerable success in his work he unfortunately continued to speculate, and according to his son it was his embarrassed circumstances which led him to consider emigrating. Certainly the family did not set out for Australia as an affluent family.

But there was another reason for considering a warmer climate. Elizabeth had borne seven children in thirteen years, and though the youngest was now twelve, she was certainly not well. Her daughter, writing home to George after Elizabeth's death in a letter which he later published, speaks of the 'illness we had flattered ourselves the voyage would remove'. Once they had crossed the equator her illness 'returned with renewed violence, and from that time she daily wasted to a shadow'. The sea voyage and presumed expertise of her husband and stepson had failed to save her.

14

Matilda does not mention tuberculosis in her letter but she describes the disease so frequently and so vividly in her fictions that it is reasonable to assume that this is what Elizabeth succumbed to. Elizabeth's father Benjamin Jacob had also died of the disease. In *Marian*, her first novel, Matilda wrote of a heroine who was tending a young girl whose lungs were already infected and who was soon to die. It appears as if the heightened emotion and the reference to the 'beloved mother' were provoked by the narrator's mention of the disease, and that Matilda was remembering the death of her own mother.

> Who could so gently raise the weary, aching head, so softly smooth the pillow, so quietly move about the chamber of the invalid, as Marian? She had bought her experience at a dear school—the bedside of a beloved mother; and sometimes, as she flitted about the room of her little pupil, preparing cooling drinks and rendering more palatable the bitter potion, or moderating the light, that its glare might not affect the sufferer, her eyes would fill with tears at recollections that would come of the *one other* time when her whole soul went forth in her occupation, as if life or death depended on her tender nursing.
>
> *Marian*, p. 123

Both Henry and Elizabeth were devout Baptists and both had experienced conversions. Little is known of the lives of their three youngest children, but the strong religious bent of Matilda, Henry John and Emily says much for the influence of their parents. Matilda's fourteen novels expressly set out to convey 'clear gospel truths … with the blessing of the Holy Spirit upon them', (as she wrote in the Preface to *Vermont Vale*), Henry became a lay preacher and an elder of the Presbyterian Church, and Emily left money in her will to the Bible Society. George, the half-brother who remained in England, was strongly connected with the Baptist Church all his life, and published Bible Acrostics and Bible Lessons as well as *Gems of Song for the Sunday School*, which went into nine editions between 1869 and 1874.

The Congreves no doubt chose to come to Adelaide primarily because two of their sons had already emigrated to South Australia. Henry John, then aged nineteen, and William, aged sixteen, had sailed in the *Trafalgar* on 20 October 1848, and had arrived at Port

Adelaide on 17 January 1849. They were assisted immigrants, each paying £6[1] for his passage, and they described themselves as chemist's assistants. Henry had been articled to a doctor at the age of fifteen, and for five years had worked with the poor in London —but perhaps nineteen-year-old doctors were unlikely candidates for assisted passages! Henry and William had chosen South Australia because the Reverend John Baptist Austin, at whose school in London Henry had completed his education and who had emigrated to South Australia in 1843, sent them a copy of *The South Australian Register* (hereafter *The Register*) containing an article which described the fine prospects available there for young men. Henry was something of an adventurer, and had previously considered emigrating to Mexico or Brazil, but the article from *The Register* turned his attention to South Australia. His letters home must have been encouraging, for according to his sketch 'My Dog Jessie', published in February 1881 in *The Adelaide Observer* (hereafter *The Observer*), he was very much enjoying his life in South Australia.

In 1852 the rest of the family decided to follow him, no doubt anticipating a reunion with the Austin family and believing that the religious climate of the colony, with its strong proportion of Dissenters, would suit them. Austin was a Congregationalist minister who had settled in the Macclesfield area, and he had much in

---

1 It is impossible to give present-day equivalents of nineteenth-century money, there are so many variables involved. I have tried by mentioning money in context frequently to allow a picture of comparative values to emerge. Inflation was low in those days, so that values remained pretty much the same during Matilda's lifetime, although the gold rushes had a marked, but temporary, effect on the price of labour and goods. G.B. Wilkinson in *The Working Man's Handbook to South Australia*, published in 1849, said that a house of brick or stone with six good rooms could be built for £40. £40 was the base stipend for a teacher paid by the Board of Education when Matilda first began to teach in Adelaide—it was believed by the Inspector to be inadequate. When the Congreves arrived in 1852 a cabbage could be bought for a penny (1d.). There were twelve pennies in a shilling (1s.) and twenty shillings in a pound (£1); £1 would have bought 240 cabbages. Later the price varied between 1d. and 2d. A two-pound loaf of bread (a quarter heavier than our standard loaf) cost between 2d. and 3½d. during Matilda's years. William Harcus in *A Handbook for Emigrants Proceeding to South Australia*, published in 1873, had 'no hesitation in saying that a man, his wife, and four children, can live in South Australia as no working people would think of living in England for about 25s. a week'.

common with Henry Congreve. He had lived in Peckham, and he was interested and skilled in medicine. At that time Congregationalists and Baptists differed little from each other. His son, also John Baptist, was the same age as Matilda. He had married three months before the Congreves arrived and lived in North Adelaide near where the Congreves were to settle.

They came as assisted immigrants, though Henry was over-age and had to pay £32 for himself, his wife and James, who at twelve was still considered a child. He gave his occupation as chemist. Frederick, who although only fourteen was described in the shipping lists as a man, is also listed as a chemist. Matilda and Emily paid £4 each (a full fare in the same class was about £25) and described themselves as servants in one list and as needlewomen in another. Teachers and governesses—which is what they were destined, and very likely determined, to become—were not acceptable occupations at the time for assisted immigrants, as the colony was oversupplied. No doubt both Matilda and Emily could sew, but it is clear from Matilda's novels that in her eyes servants in South Australia, though they might well be kind at heart, were not educated English but uneducated Irish girls. Emily's story 'Emigrating' suggests that she was appalled at having to consider herself a servant.

The Congreve family were among the 200 assisted immigrants who sailed in the steerage in the *Chatham* on 18 March 1852. Travelling steerage must have been a humiliating experience for these two gently-raised devout Baptist girls. Matilda apparently put the experience behind her. Minnie of *Minnie's Mission*, the only one of her heroines to be shown on board ship, has her passage paid by her uncle and travels in comfort in the cabin, but Emily gives a horrifying account of steerage life in 'Emigrating'.

They arrived at Port Adelaide on 1 July. It must have been a sad arrival. Elizabeth had died peacefully on the ship just out of Cape Town and had been buried at sea. Henry was far from well. In fact Dr Mayo, the doctor on board the *Chatham*, described his condition as dangerous. Port Adelaide, the landfall they had been so much desiring, was not at all attractive. 'What a barren, wretched, forlorn looking place,' was Emily's comment, in

'Emigrating', and even Matilda, when writing about an arrival at the Port some years afterwards in *Minnie's Mission*, admitted that it was then 'but a miserable disgrace to our fair land'. But, being Matilda, she added that 'sunshine does much to beautify and refresh what would often look very blank and desolate without it'.

But at last they had arrived. The voyage had taken three months and thirteen days.

CHAPTER 2

What Can an Educated Woman Do But Teach?

They rented a house in Finniss Street, North Adelaide, then an unfashionable street. It was a three-roomed house of brick and stone near Brougham Place, not far from Kermode Street where the young John Baptist Austin was living. It could not have been much of a house as its rateable value was only £20, though values at the time were low, the gold rushes having left one house in five empty. Letters home to England from his sisters told George that soon after arrival Henry was dangerously ill. For six weeks he was near death, although he did eventually recover. It must have been during this very worrying time that Matilda took the first steps to consolidate their position. According to her family, although she was of a quiet and gentle nature, she was a woman of great drive and determination. In a city deprived of men by the gold rushes, her brothers Henry and William included, she must make her way, and perhaps that of the whole family. Although nothing is known of her childhood and youth it is clear that she was well-educated. Like her brother Henry who was only eighteen months her junior, she had probably been taught at home by her mother. Elizabeth Congreve was a scholarly woman and Henry later wrote that he had had the privilege of a good education, which included Greek and Latin, at his mother's hands. Matilda was certainly well-read. This is obvious from the number and nature of the writers she quotes and refers to in her writings. It seems reasonable to believe that she had had some experience of teaching at home in England, at least in Sabbath schools. Now she did what seemed the most sensible thing. She opened a school at their home, and applied to become a licensed teacher.

This was not an easy undertaking. There was no point in applying for a licence to teach unless a school of at least twenty pupils, but preferably nearer thirty, between the ages of six and sixteen, was already in existence. The parents of the children had to certify their intention to place their children in the school, and a Justice of the Peace had to certify that the names of the parents were those of *bona fide* residents, that the teacher was in every way fit to undertake the care and instruction of the pupils, and that proper accommodation was provided for the school. Most schools at that time were held of necessity in unsuitable rooms in private houses, with inadequate books, furniture, space and ventilation.

The records of the Central Board of Education show that Matilda's first school was in Finniss Street, North Adelaide, and it seems inevitable therefore that it was held in a room in the house which the family had taken. Some of their small capital had surely been used to furnish, however meagrely, this little school. Ten years earlier Henry Hussey's mother had opened a school after merely 'procuring two or three forms for seats'.

Matilda's application for a teacher's licence had been received by the Board of Education by 25 September 1852. She had worked very hard indeed. In less than three months after her arrival in Adelaide she had fulfilled all the requirements: she had twenty-four children on her books, had the necessary memorials from parents and certifications from the Justice of the Peace, she had written to the Board and was waiting for the arrival of the Inspector on whose favourable report her livelihood depended. The Inspector arrived, and reported that he had found twenty-four children present and the school 'efficiently conducted'. The licence was granted, but it was not backdated. For her first difficult weeks she was paid nothing by the Board of Education. A teacher's stipend was at that time £40 per annum, paid quarterly, and Matilda was paid only for the last quarter of 1852.

The pay was not good. The Inspector often reported that he thought teachers were underpaid, and in fact those considered to be the better teachers were frequently paid £60. When the Board had sufficient funds bonuses were given which had the effect of boosting the stipends of the teachers in the most successful city schools to over £100 per annum. Success was measured largely by location and attendance. There was some justice in this, at least as far as attendance was concerned; only teachers who could make their pupils feel that school was worthwhile were likely to retain them.

Indeed attendance was always a problem. An attendance book had to be kept (issued by the Board, but at the teacher's expense) and monthly returns verified before a Justice of the Peace. Unfortunately attendance was always spasmodic, for children who were needed at home were kept at home—and of course many were needed. (This was a considerable problem in the country as Matilda must have found later when she moved to the Mount Barker area.)

It is true that teachers could add to their incomes by charging an additional sixpence or shilling a week for each child, if the parents were willing and able to pay. But parents would keep home for the rest of the week a child who was ill for two or three days in order to avoid payment for that week. Only those children who attended each month for twenty days of at least three hours were reckoned for payment. On average, parents paid £1 or just over each year for each child. These payments formed a considerable part of the teacher's income but they could not be enforced. Naturally teachers in wealthier areas were the better paid.

The Inspector frequently complained that not only was attendance erratic but many pupils were up to an hour late each day. This must have been a nightmare for the teachers, both in teaching and in keeping attendance records. As well, there was much sickness in unhygienic areas where people lived crowded together, and in crowded schoolrooms too. And there were few holidays— only three weeks at Christmas, one week at Midwinter, and Friday and Monday at Easter. The extra holiday for the Queen's Birthday must have been much appreciated in those days.

There were other problems associated with conducting a school. Until the Board began supplying books several years later—textbooks graded to suit various levels of attainment—it was very difficult to organise pupils into classes. Children as young as four might be sent. Others might be fifteen or sixteen. Some would know their alphabet, having been taught at home—the Inspector believed that all children should be taught their alphabet by their parents before they were sent to school, but of course many were not. Books and slates had to be supplied by the teachers. There was no curriculum or training. Teachers taught from memories of their own schooldays. The only requirement from the Board was that there must be readings from the Old Testament and the New Testament twice daily. This at least must have pleased Matilda. Another problem was competition for students. When Matilda opened her first school there were twenty Board schools in the City of Adelaide, and two others in North Adelaide, but within a year the number of schools in North Adelaide had increased to seven.

Running a school was at the best of times a precarious existence, and for Matilda, sorrowing deeply for her mother, in a new country with few friends, and with a father seriously ill, it must have been very difficult indeed. But it was evidently what Matilda saw as the best, and probably the only, way for her to make a living. As she was later to make her character Beatrice Melton say in similar circumstances:

> … leaving our dear father's grave behind us, we came here to commence our new life. There was but one thing to be done; what is there, indeed, that an educated woman *can* do but teach? There is so little left for them in the struggle for life. Thank God that so many can do this, well and efficiently.
>
> *Beatrice Melton's Discipline*, p. 11

By the beginning of December the future was looking much brighter. Matilda's school was well established, she was being paid, and her father's health was improving. On the evening of Friday 17 December he walked with his sons Frederick and James from their home in Finniss Street to the South Australian Company's mill at Hackney and was in high spirits, singing favourite hymns as they returned.

The next morning, however, one of the boys called Matilda to him and she found him breathing very heavily. Dr Davies from Kermode Street was called but he was too late—Henry was dead when he arrived. A post mortem examination was made, and an inquest was held the same afternoon at the British Tavern in Finniss Street. The jury found that Henry had died by the 'Visitation of God'. Dr Davies reported that he had died of a ruptured aorta and added that it would have been impossible for him to have lived much longer. An interesting sidelight is thrown upon the times by the account of the inquest given in *The Adelaide Morning Chronicle*, which pointed out that considerable difficulty had occurred in forming a jury because a number of those summoned for service had failed to turn up. The Coroner George Stevenson announced his intention of fining in future any juror who, having been summoned, failed to appear.

It must have been a sad Christmas for the young people, and things did not improve in the new year. Their difficulties were in fact compounded. It seems that they were no longer able to afford to keep the house in Finniss Street—though the rent charged for a £20 house would not have been much—and Matilda was having troubles with her school. The inspector who visited the school in April reported that it was 'inferior', which in the circumstances is not really surprising. ('Inferior' meant that she was having trouble in sustaining numbers.)

In May Matilda wrote to the Board of Education for permission to move her school to Kermode Street, where two doors away from the residence of John Austin there was an empty chapel, a brick building which could be used as a school, and which was not subject to rates. Permission was given, conditional upon the increased efficiency of the school.

It is possible that it was a good move. There was an epidemic of some kind in the winter of 1853 and many children in the Adelaide and North Adelaide areas died. A larger chapel building would certainly have been a healthier place to conduct a school than a small room in a private house. And Kermode Street was a better address. It was at that time the main street of North Adelaide.

They left Finniss Street, and since their names do not appear anywhere in the rate assessment lists in 1853 it is reasonable to assume that they went into lodgings. Many of Matilda's characters live in lodgings, and so does Emily's Cary. In fact it seems possible that they lodged not far from Kermode Street in Margaret Street where cheap lodgings could be had at that time, for although not often identifying places by name in their stories they both write of people living in lodgings in Margaret Street, and both give vivid descriptions.

Henry, Matilda's brother, said that in spite of these difficulties Matilda managed to keep the family together. Emily probably helped in the school, although a bitter little section of her story 'Little Cary's Experiences as a "New Chum"' suggests that for a time while they were in Adelaide she may have had experience as a nursery governess. A reader certainly receives the impression that she is writing from experience. Perhaps this happened after the death of their father.

James and Frederick (one assumes) attended Matilda's school until their education was complete or until they were able to find jobs. Little is known of the later lives of these two young men. Frederick was at different times in his life a teacher for the Board of Education at Condowie, a private tutor, a prospector and a mining correspondent. He spent a year in New Zealand and four years in Victoria. James, according to his brother Henry, was 'highly gifted'. In 1864 he was 'away roaming the world and no tidings ever reach our anxious ears'. However in 1885 he was in Adelaide, in touch with Matilda, and in 1899 at the time of the death of his nephew Henry Congreve Evans, Matilda's son, he was in South Australia probably living with William at Bridgewater. He later went to Sydney.

The school in Kermode Street did not last for long. And yet Matilda was doing well in her new bigger premises. When the inspector called in March 1854 she had thirteen boys and thirty-three girls in her school—this was one of the biggest attendances in the whole of the area of Adelaide and North Adelaide. It is impossible to know what prompted her to leave the city. Perhaps she believed that life in the country would be cheaper or healthier; perhaps the boys, or one of them, gained employment in the country; perhaps the boys left home and Matilda thought life might be better under the protection of Reverend John Baptist Austin, who at the time was living on his property 'Lashbrooke' at Macclesfield, and conducting services there and at other centres in the area including Mount Barker, or perhaps she had heard of the vacancy at the 'Yunkunga' school. She might have heard of this from the Reverend J.B. Austin. At any rate, at the beginning of April 1854, when she had been teaching at the school in Kermode Street for just less than a year (and was usually reported by the inspector as being 'tolerably efficient'), she wrote to the Board of Education resigning her licence to teach there and explaining that she intended to apply for a licence to teach at Mount Barker. (A Mrs Burt took over Matilda's school almost immediately which suggests that it was a successful school and that Matilda cared about what happened to her pupils and took pains to arrange a successor.) The Board accepted her resignation but pointed out that she would be unlikely to be granted a licence for Mount Barker as a school had just been licensed there. Nevertheless the Kermode Street school was closed on 19 April and Matilda moved to the Mount Barker area.

CHAPTER 3

Country Life

Matilda did not apply for the Mount Barker school. There was a vacancy for a teacher at 'Yunkunga', the property of Walter Paterson, about five kilometres southeast of the Mount Barker township, near what is now Wistow. The Reverend W. Gray, whose article in *The Mount Barker Courier* on 27 June 1930 about 'The Authoress Maud Jean Franc' has in the past been much relied on for information about Matilda, says that 'one of her first engagements [in South Australia] was to go as a governess to the Walter Paterson family'. No doubt the fact that Matilda's first novel *Marian* had a governess to a family on a 'farmstead fifty miles up the country' as its heroine helped to give credence to this story. It can hardly be true, however, as Walter Paterson's children were all too old to need a governess by the time Matilda moved to the area. The term 'governess' was frequently used as a synonym for schoolteacher, which of course was what Matilda was at Yunkunga, a licensed teacher paid by the Board of Education. However, Mr Paterson was a public-spirited man who contributed to the well-being of the district in many ways and it seems likely that he, as others elsewhere had done, was willing to provide facilities for a school on his property. No Board of Education school was built in the Mount Barker area for many years after this.

In his article on Matilda, Gray reported that 'Mr Paterson built for her a slab room on the south end of his Kunyunga [*sic*] property. The size of it, traceable in the foundations, was about 20 × 15 ft., with a great half-circular fire place, that occupied the west end of this school room.' This very likely refers to a schoolroom built by Mr Paterson for the use of the local teacher and local scholars. It is also possible that Matilda—and perhaps Emily, whom Gray reports, wrongly, as always being with Matilda and acting as the music teacher in her schools—lodged with Walter Paterson's family while she was schoolmistress at Yunkunga, and that this gave rise to the story that she had been governess to his family. She would have needed to live near the school. But it is much more likely that there was a minute dwelling attached to the schoolroom. In an earlier article in *The Mount Barker Courier*, this time on Walter Paterson, Gray remarked that 'The remains of a circular fireplace built by Mr Paterson in the house in which [Miss Congreve] and her sister lived, survives the wearing effects of time.'

Walter Paterson certainly took a great interest in the Yunkunga school and in the teacher—and yet it seems as though there was some problem there. The teacher whose move had created the vacancy filled by Matilda was Henry Bonnar. The first teacher of the Yunkunga school, he had been there only one quarter when he resigned because of ill health, yet within two months he had applied for a licence to teach at Mount Barker Springs. Matilda lasted eighteen months at Yunkunga, and on her resignation Mr Paterson wrote to the Board saying that it was the wish of himself and others that the Board would license a male teacher rather than a female teacher for the school at Yunkunga. The Board's reply—that there was 'much doubt as to whether the neighbourhood would furnish materials for a school that would at all remunerate a male teacher'—throws an interesting sidelight on the difficulties experienced by single women such as Matilda.

The Board eventually licensed a Mr Melville, but he too did not stay: in fact he left 'without notice', and by May 1857 Mr Paterson was again writing to the Board appealing for a teacher at Yunkunga. Two other teachers (both males) came for short periods but by the end of 1860 the school was abandoned altogether. Given the obvious problem in keeping a teacher in the area one wonders why Paterson was so anxious not to have a female teacher again.

The tone of her first novel *Marian* suggests that Matilda was happy in the area. She responded whole-heartedly to the idea of farm life, but of course it may not have been from Mr Paterson's farm that she learnt what that life was like. Maybe he thought that rough farm boys were too much for a young girl to handle. However, considering the way that she always maintained numbers in her school when many other teachers (including, as we shall see, her brother and her husband) had very great difficulty, it seems that Matilda was a competent teacher.

Paterson of course was a widower. His wife had died in 1842, leaving him with five little children. In 1855 he was forty-four, and his children were grown-up or nearly grown-up. Perhaps the presence of two unmarried young ladies on his property was an embarrassment—or even a distraction! Nevertheless Paterson certainly influenced Matilda in one way. He was renowned for his knowledge of phrenology, and frequently lectured on the subject, 'causing much amusement by his manipulation of the cranium'. This seems to have rubbed off on Matilda, for there are many references—usually playful—to the 'bumps' or 'organs' of characters, particularly in her early novels. When Martin Wallace of *Golden Gifts* sets out to find a female servant he remarks that he knows Australian servants are not remarkable for the 'organ of order' but makes it clear that he intends to 'look out for a regular elevation of that bump, my dear Lizzie; nothing short of a young mountain will satisfy me'.

Whatever the problems at Yunkunga Matilda appears again to have had some success as a teacher, though as usual like most teachers she had problems with the Board. She sometimes had as many as thirty-five pupils, though once as few as eighteen. There were usually more girls than boys, but that was only to be expected in a farming district. She applied for a licence in early July, a couple of months after she left Kermode Street, but the Inspector was slow to arrive.

By 20 September she was pleading with the Board to be allowed to forward returns with a view to obtaining a licence. She now had thirty-four pupils, which was a large school at the time. In October she was still awaiting the Inspector's visit and complaining of difficulties arising from the lack of school books. The Board did not help with the books, but in November the Inspector finally arrived and found her school to be 'tolerably efficient'. She was granted a licence backdated to 1 July. She must have been relieved, for she had surely suffered substantially from the lack of a steady income.

She stayed there another year. It is clear that she loved the area, for it is celebrated so obviously and so lovingly in *Marian*, the novel she was soon to write and which she may indeed have begun there. Emily was almost certainly with her at this time. According to the Reverend W. Gray, local residents remembered that she had helped in Matilda's schools. Some of Emily's poems survive in manuscript and Mount Barker is mentioned in them.

In the second week of January 1856 Matilda resigned and her name disappeared from the records of the Board of Education for a few months. Surprisingly the name of her brother William now appeared. William had arrived in South Australia with Henry in 1849 and I have been able to discover little of what he had been doing. He had been briefly at the goldfields with Henry and had spent most of his time in Victoria. Maybe he returned to South Australia with the idea of setting up house with Matilda and Emily, or perhaps indeed with Emily alone. He and Emily were close in age—he was eighteen months younger—and they may well have once been special friends. Many of Emily's stories feature a close relationship between a brother and sister.

In any event he did not take over the vacant Yunkunga school but endeavoured to set up a new school at Bugle Ranges, a place incidentally not far from 'Lashbrooke' the residence of the Reverend John Baptist Austin. It is possible, even probable, that Matilda or Emily or perhaps both of them were with him at this time. Unfortunately he had great difficulty in enrolling a sufficient number of pupils to qualify for a licence, although the Board was very sympathetic and did eventually backdate his licence to 1 April 1856. Clearly it was very difficult for him to sustain numbers. The parents of the children in this farming community were constantly removing their children at busy times like seedtime and harvest.

By the middle of 1857 he had given up, admitting that the area could not sustain a school, and although there was already another vacancy at Yunkunga where the new teacher had resigned, he told the Board that he had hopes of setting up a school at Langhorne's Creek. An application form was sent to him with the Board's blessing, and in the next few months there was much correspondence between the Board and the citizens of Langhorne's Creek about the building of a schoolhouse. When the school opened in February 1858, however, William was not the licensed teacher. It seems likely that he had given up the struggle and returned to Victoria where there was a shortage of teachers, and that he remained there until his retirement.

Once William was established in his school Matilda took steps to re-establish herself. By the early August of 1856 she had applied for a licence for a school in the heart of Mount Barker on the west side of Hutchinson Street, just north of Gawler Street, where she had 'collected a school of about thirty pupils'. This time she was unwilling to wait so long for the Board to respond, and Mr John Austin wrote a letter to the Board recommending her as a fit person. It did not work, however; it was November before she received her licence and then it was backdated only to 1 November 1856. Another three months without a stipend!

Emily perhaps waited to see how William would fare. Maybe she helped him at first—in one of her stories she tells of a sister assisting her brother to set up a school. But when it became clear that a school could not be sustained at Bugle Ranges she must have decided that she must make her own way. She moved back to the plains, to Prospect Village, an area not far from the present Prospect Oval, and from 1 October 1857 was licensed to teach there.

There had been a school at Prospect Village but it had closed some years before, and Emily's school is listed as being in a new locality. She did not therefore take over an established school but had to work to get her school together. The Inspector's report said of her school that it was 'A small elementary school, in a thinly-populated district, fairly conducted'. Not the sort of school, one imagines, to draw the bonuses and higher stipend that were given to successful city teachers. She remained there until her resignation on 15 July 1861.

It must have been at about this time—perhaps at Christmas 1856, or perhaps at Christmas 1857—that the family reunion so vividly described by their brother Henry took place. Writing in *The Inglewood Advertiser* in December 1864, under the pseudonym of 'Honricus', Henry reflected on his fifteen Christmases in Australia, and on the last Christmas in England, spent at his brother George's house: 'That last meeting I shall never forget—father, mother, sisters and brothers, were all gathered—where are they now?' He writes sadly of the death of his parents and of the scattering of the family. But one Christmas in Australia stands out. Clearly this reunion had taken place some years before, and the details suggest that it is likely to have happened during the time that Matilda had her house in Mount Barker.

> The Christmas, the happiest of all in my colonial experience, was spent under the roof of my sister, in South Australia. I had arrived late on Christmas eve from the Victorian diggings, and being tired had gone early to bed. I was awoke in the morning by the tones of a piano, which gave utterance to those beautiful 'Bird Waltzes', and I lay for some time entranced, sweet visions of home came gushing over my mind, and I wept. At the breakfast table we assembled a happy group, brothers and sisters gathered from all parts of the island. The soft morning breeze came in through the open windows, bringing with it the sweets it had stolen from a thousand flowers in the surrounding garden. Changes we had to speak of, histories to exchange, and it was delightful as thought after thought came out, to recognise the likeness of mind, to that which we remembered years ago, before our long separation. Faces and forms had changed, but the mind was unaltered, matured it is true, but still preserving the impress which had been first laid upon it. Then there was the gathering together in the evening, the visits of hearty neighbours, the glancing of loveable eyes, the social chat, the music, and the final walk amongst the old gums, while the bright moon sailed overhead and cast flickering shadows from the boughs across our pathway.

Matilda stayed at the Mount Barker School for well over three years. It was her most settled period to date in Australia, and there are indications that she was comfortable with what she was doing. She had sufficient leisure to be able to transmute the experience of the last few years into a novel. Her school suited her—it was virtually a girls' school, with twenty-eight girls and only one or two boys. She had taken a house and was hoping to extend her school to include boarders. Almost weekly, from 23 October 1858 until 30 June 1859, she advertised the fact in *The South Australian Weekly Chronicle*: 'A Happy Home and a Careful Education. Terms moderate (adapted to the times), may be known on application to Miss Congreve, Mount Barker.'

That she had at least two resident pupils seems likely, since from the time the new Presbyterian Church in Hutchinson Street opened in the middle of 1858 until her departure from Mount Barker in early 1860 she rented three places in a pew. (Mr Walter Paterson rented two places while Matilda was there, but when she left, he left! He had been a prime mover in the establishment of the church, having been secretary of the appeal fund as well as a contributor to it).

We are unlikely ever to discover who sat in the two extra places. I cannot believe that James and Frederick still lived with Matilda. In 1858 they were aged nineteen and twenty-one and like Henry and William they were adventurers and roamers. It is tempting to think that the two people who accompanied her to church on Sundays were the two young children of Mr E. Evans, schoolteacher of Nuriootpa, whose wife had died suddenly at the beginning of the year. They were very young—Mary Ann was three-and-a-half, and Ebenezer just past two—but Matilda does tell, in a story written much later, of a widower who sends his young children to live at the home of a country schoolteacher whom he later marries. We shall never know.

What we do know is that on 16 February 1860 Matilda Jane Congreve, third daughter of Mr Henry Congreve of Peckham, Surrey, married Ephraim Evans, Baptist Minister of Nuriootpa, at the Zion Chapel in Pulteney Street, Adelaide. The marriage seems to have been sudden, for the pew in the Presbyterian Church had been rented for the first quarter of 1860, and the Board of Education did not receive Matilda's resignation until four days after the marriage. She did, however, showing her concern for her students, recommend that Mrs Ann Tapley, formerly of the school at Enfield, succeed her at Mount Barker, a recommendation which the Board accepted.

Marriage changed her life dramatically, but before looking at the life of Matilda Jane Evans, we should look at the birth of Maud Jeanne Franc, because it is by that name that she became known in the colony and in other states and countries. (She first spelled the second name Jean, but later it appeared as Jeanne, and as that is the form which has been adopted by Australian librarians and bibliographers it is the form which I shall use.)

CHAPTER 4

Marian *and* Maud Jeanne Franc

In 1859, when *Marian* was published, Matilda must have been feeling cheerful and confident about life. She had overcome the problems associated with her parents' deaths, she had an established position in Mount Barker, a place which she loved, and she had shown herself to be innovative, even adventurous, in attempting to write a novel about South Australia. No doubt she suffered financial difficulties, especially as the Board of Education so often refused to licence her for the months of teaching which occurred before the arrival of the Inspector. But the fact that she could afford the places in the Presbyterian Church, and that she had the confidence to place in a paper like *The South Australian Weekly Chronicle* an eye-catching advertisement offering a 'happy home' and a 'careful education' to boarding pupils suggests that she was feeling herself at last in control of her life.

The first part of *Marian, or The Light of Someone's Home, A Tale of Australian Bush Life*, came out in June 1859, but of course she must have begun it some time before. E. H. Hallack, writing a series of articles on farming and township life in *The Observer* in 1892, commented, after a visit to Walter Paterson who was by then a local identity, that she wrote it while she was living at Yunkunga. It is certainly about that area. Hallack mentions that Sheoak Hill, which fronted Paterson's property, 'obtained notoriety through having been mentioned in the well-known novel entitled "Marian, or the Light of Some-one's Home"'. In the novel Marian climbs Sheoak Hill and describes the view which can be seen from it. 'To her right hand, meeting the clear horizon, the glassy waters of a lake were visible.' Yunkunga Road is still to be found today, running past the old Eden Park homestead. A little further on, where the road now is known as Hender Road, the old Yunkunga home section can be seen on the right, with the little creek in front and the hill behind it. Opposite it on the left, now capped with pines, not sheoaks, can be seen what must have been Sheoak Hill. At its base there are still some grand old sheoaks, and from the top of the hill, just as Marian saw them, the waters of Lake Alexandrina can be seen meeting the horizon. That there is so much about this area in *Marian* does suggest that it may have been begun there. But it was surely finished in Mount Barker at a time when she was well-known to its residents and tradespeople, and was getting to know an up-and-coming local printer.

The four little volumes, issued monthly from June to September, which make up this first novel of Maud Jeanne Franc are charming if rather flimsy little books, which bring back a past world when one holds them in one's hand. They are quite small— 11 × 18.4 centimetres—and their paper covers are of different colours. The first two parts of the copy in the Mitchell library have pale blue covers, the third is yellow and the fourth a pinky orange. The parts of the National Library's copy are all different from these: the first pinky brown, the second green, the third rose, and the fourth yellow. This suggests that when the parts were offered for sale in local bookshops they had an attractively varied appearance, which allowed readers the satisfaction of choosing what best pleased them. The little volumes contain advertisements, so that some of the cost of publication could be defrayed, but of course the advertisements were not retained when the parts were bound.

The place of publication was given as Mount Barker. Alfred Waddy, publisher and printer, had premises in Gilles Street, Mount Barker, and the other publisher, William Hallows Hillier in Adelaide. An Adelaide connection would have been vital for the success of the enterprise. Nevertheless Hillier was not the only Adelaide business interested, for the many advertisements for the parts in Adelaide papers always state that they can be bought 'at all booksellers'.

Something of the progress of *Marian* in the estimation of the publishers and the public can be gauged by noting the changes in the information given as part succeeded part. In the second part the name of the Melbourne firm Gordon and Gotch had been added to the list of publishers. Part three carried a notice advising that 'This work has a wide and increasing circulation in this and the adjoining colonies' and noted that Waddy was removing to bigger premises. Part four announced that Alfred Waddy's premises were now at 13 and 14 Gawler Street, then and now the main street of Mount Barker. In addition, either through contacts of the Australian publishers, or with the assistance of Matilda's half-brother George, a fourth and very important publisher had been found: Binns and Goodwin, London and Bath. Part three had announced that there would be five parts, but in the end there were only four, and part four ended with the preliminary pages necessary for those wishing to have the parts bound—the title page, carrying the names of all four publishers, a preface by the Authoress, dated Mount Barker, September 1859, and a table of contents. An advertisement announced that John Howell, stationer, was also acting as an outlet in Adelaide. So much can be gleaned from these little copies.

Other sources reveal that *Marian* had met with such success that a second edition had been needed early on. It must have been satisfying to Waddy and his co-publishers to need to place advertisements in *The Register* asking agents to return unsold copies because the part was out of print and awaiting reprinting. By mid October advertisements in *The Register* announced that the parts could be taken to Waddy or Hillier to be bound for 2s. 6d. per volume.

The author's preface appeared only after all four parts had been issued and the book was ready for binding. Early reviews of the first part noted that 'our authoress has launched her literary venture without one word of preface, introduction, or explanation of any kind whatever'. There was however a statement in part one from the publisher which was sufficiently explanatory of the purposes of the book and has something to tell us now about how the reading of novels was regarded at the time. It also suggests what there was in the book which the publisher believed would make it a commercial proposition.

> Among the many publications that adorn our Periodical Literature, the publishers are not aware of any that treat exclusively on South Australian Subjects. It is presumed that a work professing to supply that void, may meet with a favourable reception. To the ordinary Novel many objections have been raised, some of them of a grave nature: it is hoped that this little work will be obnoxious to none of them. Although seeking to amuse a vacant hour, its principal object is to elevate the mind, improve the heart, and develope the graces of mental training based on a foundation of vital religion.
>
> Should these objects be accomplished it will be a source of gratification to the Publishers that they have contributed, in however small a degree, to the amusement and perhaps advantage of the Reader.

Clearly the publishers hoped that its exclusively South Australian setting and subject matter would give it a ready sale in that state, and they believed that it was such a mild, pure, moral and religious novel that the prejudices against novel reading, which had been fuelled at that time by the popularity of 'sensation' novels, would be set aside as readers realised that the book would be a positive influence for good.

The author's preface, when it came, was disarming. Its style—of a kind which used to be called 'flowery'—is very much of its time. But its point is clear. The author is full of love for the people around her, as she is indeed for the characters in her book, and she believes that what she has written is remarkable only for its simplicity and truth to life.

To The Reader

> We have ventured in all love and confidence, to cast among the thousand lovely flowers of the parterre, our simple little wild blossom for your acceptance. We have no hope of winning your favour by brilliancy of color—grace of form—or rich and rare perfume, yet has our little wildling higher aspirations—it hopes by its simplicity and truthfulness to gain your heart, it seeks an entrance to your affections by the very faintness of its fragrance.

We have sought to place before you, that which is most
lovely, most pure, most undefiled. We have been actuated by a
sincere desire to exhibit the beauty of true *Religion* as exemplified in the daily walk of life. It has been our aim to show how
pleasant are 'Wisdom's ways,' even amidst earth's constant
interchange of joy and sorrow.

If, however feebly, something of this shall be attained; if, in
any measure, we may cause you to see one beauty in Religion
hitherto unknown, or raise the faintest aspiration after that
'Holiness without which no man shall see the Lord:' then more
than realized will be our highest hopes.

Marian herself, the main character, was the author's vehicle to
demonstrate the beauty of true Religion in daily life.

The claims which are made in the Preface were taken up by
the English publishers when they first advertised the first English
edition in *The Publishers' Circular*, the London book trade journal
published by Sampson and Low. There was more than one publisher. Just as Waddy had used other firms to help market *Marian*
in Australia, Binns and Goodwin did the same in England. Binns
and Goodwin of Bath were the printers of the first English edition,
but with their names on the title page appear also the names of
R.E. Peach—about whom I have discovered nothing at all—A.
Waddy, Mount Barker, South Adelaide [*sic!*], and a London firm,
Darton & Co.

When the first advertisement for this new Australian novel
appeared in *The Publishers' Circular* on 15 September 1860 the
publishers stated that they believed that they were dealing with a
'remarkable work'. The fact that it 'emanated from Australia'
made it especially interesting. They believed in its truthfulness
and quoted from the review in *The Register*: 'Delicacy and good
taste pervade every page. All the hopes and fears that sway the
characters of this tale are precisely such as may be witnessed in
numberless houses on this broad continent'. They announced the
publication date of 1 October and asked for orders 'without delay'.

When *Myra*, a novel by another early Australian woman
writer, Louisa Atkinson, of New South Wales, was republished in
1988, an introduction by Victor Crittenden gives what is I suspect
a widely held view about the publication prospects of early

Australian writers, especially women.

> The novels by Louisa were written for an Australian audience
> and they never received the imprimatur of an English publish-
> er, not because they were not good enough but their subjects
> lacked the special appeal needed for English success. They
> were not spectacular in the display of characters and seldom
> exotic enough in their settings. Louisa taking the landscape for
> granted rarely giving detailed descriptions usually failed to
> include such dramatic events as bushfires and attacks by abo-
> rigines.

It is worth pointing out that these limitations did not prevent
Matilda from finding an overseas publisher. She too wrote for an
Australian audience; indeed, even more narrowly she wrote, at
least in *Marian*, for a South Australian audience. Her novels are
never spectacular in characters or incidents; in one of her later
novels *No Longer A Child* she expressly stated that she believed
that there was enough in 'civilized, every-day, practical life' to
make readable stories, and that writing of 'the feats of the bush-
ranger' or the ' "stock-in-trade" native and aboriginal incidents'
was only 'to pander to the sensational taste of the day' (p. 72).

Yet all her novels were eventually published in London, and
they proved popular. Maybe she was lucky, first in finding in
Mount Barker an enterprising publisher like Alfred Waddy, and
later in finding an English publisher ready to take her work.
Perhaps having a half-brother in England was a significant factor.

The religious purpose of her early novels certainly made it
possible to direct her work to a specialised market, both in
Australia and elsewhere. Nevertheless, although *Marian* was to
change publishers twice in the next five years, it still continued to
be issued. Darton took over from Binns and Goodwin sometime
in the early 1860s and when Darton split with another partner
Sampson Low became Matilda's publishers. They kept *Marian* in
print for the next sixty-five years. It obviously had something:
staying-power if nothing else!

But I suspect that the success of Maud Jeanne Franc as a writer
has more to do with the entrepreneurial and marketing skills of
her publishers than with the quality of her writing. *Marian* in its

day had novelty and charm; even today something of that charm can be felt. Properly marketed, it found its public. Once Matilda had found her niche she had only to go on writing, and it was worth her publishers' while to keep on publishing. Her novels, though not as good as those of Catherine Helen Spence, were conspicuously better marketed. Spence's *Clara Morison* and *Tender and True*, when they came out in 1854 and 1856, were given only very brief advertisements in *The Publishers' Circular*. *Marian* and *Vermont Vale*, Matilda's first two novels, were given large, illustrated advertisements in the Christmas numbers of the years in which they appeared.

Clara Morison was published at 9s. while the price of *Marian* was at first 6s. and by the time of the second edition 5s. Thereafter no Franc novel ever cost more than 5s. and many of them were issued at 4s. After Matilda's death there were many cheaper editions. *Tender and True* on the other hand appeared at 21s. It is no wonder that it was not to be readily found in Adelaide bookshops!

It is worth remembering that it was Sampson Low rather than Matilda who stood to gain from the fact that her novels were kept in print. Copyright laws were such at the time that the books would have been sold outright; Matilda retained copyright of only her last two novels and this she left in her will to her sons. I have no idea what money Matilda made from her literary activities. She did not die a wealthy woman, though she appears to have been comfortably off. But then she kept schools most of her life as well as continuing with her writing.

There are no records extant from the relevant publishers, but Catherine Helen Spence recorded in her *Autobiography* that she was paid £40 for the copyright of *Clara Morison*, although £10 was deducted for the abridging which the publishers deemed necessary. This did not happen to Matilda's books. Those that appeared first in Australia, either in serial or in book form, differ only in minor details from the London editions. But considering that £40 was the base stipend for a schoolteacher, £30 was a large sum of money and even £20—which is what Spence received in 1856 for *Tender and True*—would have been some compensation to Matilda for her efforts.

However, she may well have received more than this for *Marian* and her later novels. George Marston, who was a partner with Sampson Low in publishing Matilda's novels, indicated in his 1887 book on Copyright that sometimes publishers paid bonuses to authors who had sold the copyright of books which then proved popular. Nothing is known about the fees paid to Matilda for novels serialised in periodicals. Spence was paid £35 for *Mr Hogarth's Will* when it was published in book form in England, but she also received £50 from the Adelaide evening paper *The Telegraph* for its serialisation under the title *Uphill Work* in their paper *The Weekly Mail*. This gives an indication that serial publishing was worthwhile. We can only hope that Matilda felt adequately rewarded for what proved to be a life of unremitting industry.

Marian had modest success overseas, as it had had in Australia; perhaps this was partly because of its novelty. It was a genuine domestic novel, but a very different kind of domestic novel, because it was set in a part of the world where personal relationships were conducted more easily and class distinctions meant less. There was an attractive freedom and casualness about the writing.

From the first readers in England wanted it. The parts were eagerly awaited by the compositors who were setting the type; they 'vied with each other in obtaining the "copy" before it was committed to print'. Binns and Goodwin received orders for 'upwards of 800 copies' in the fortnight before publication. It came out in October and by December the second English edition was in preparation. It was given a full page advertisement featuring a large reproduction of the frontispiece in the Christmas edition of *The Publishers' Circular*, where it was fulsomely described:

> The style of this work is peculiarly natural and graceful, and while presenting to the reader an interesting account of genteel Colonial Life, and new scenes, possesses a charm that makes the close of its pages resemble the farewell to loved and honoured friends.

One thousand copies of the second edition had already been ordered by the time it came out in June 1861. The price had been reduced and the book had been improved in appearance.

> It is expected that the circulation will thus be increased of a book so deservedly esteemed, both for the simple, and genuine, and sterling interest of its pages, as well as for its truly useful influence on the character of its readers.

There was no doubt about it—*Marian, or The Light of Someone's Home*, by Maud Jeanne Franc was a success. But why did Matilda Congreve of Hutchinson Street, Mount Barker need a pseudonym, and why did she choose such an odd name as Franc? It is easy enough to understand why women chose male pseudonyms. I would like to think that Matilda showed a feminist strength in choosing a female name, but alas, a male pseudonym would have been pointless. Her novels are so very feminine that no-one surely could ever have been deceived! It may be that Miss Congreve, schoolmistress, wished to dissociate her two personalities. It seems that no attempt was ever made to hide her writing identity—from the first the Mount Barker people showed themselves proud of the achievement of their author and publisher. Nevertheless, the persona of the narrator of her stories was maybe more sure of herself and more able to reveal herself, especially in religious matters and in her exhortations about behaviour, than Miss Congreve with her quiet, gentle and unassuming personality was able to do. Two names for two different roles in life may well have been convenient.

But having decided on a pseudonym, why pick Franc? I have puzzled over this for some years, and have discovered nothing. Maud and Jeanne, (which she—or her publishers—sometimes spelled Maude and Jean in various combinations) are variants of Matilda and Jane. But Franc? In French it means free, candid, real, true, downright, or as it is spelled in English, frank. This is certainly a meaning which might have suited Matilda. Though in many ways a conventional writer she is certainly outspoken about religion and domestic behaviour. But it seems odd that she should use an adjective as a surname, and choose the masculine, not the feminine, form of the word. 'Maud Jean Franche' is certainly more logical, though it is virtually unpronounceable in English.

I wondered if Franc was perhaps a rare, but known, surname in English. My researches have shown that very few people of the name of Franc have left traces of themselves in English history. One, however, aroused my interest. Guillaume Franc (*c.* 1505-1570) was credited until recently with being the musical editor of the famous first Psalter, published at Geneva by Calvin for the use of the reformed churches. Matilda came from a musical family and her maternal grandfather, Benjamin Jacob, 'one of the best organists of his time' according to Grove's *Dictionary of Music and Musicians* (Third Edition), also edited a psalter: 'a collection of tunes, with appropriate symphonies, set to a course of psalms, and published under the title of *National Psalmody* in 1817'. Matilda, whose novels are full of hymns and psalms, surely had this book. And she may well also have had the standard history of music of the day—Charles Burney's *A General History of Music*, published between 1776 and 1789. It was there, in an account of the setting of the psalms to music, that I found a reference to Guillaume Franc: 'an obscure musician … whose name has never had admission in any catalogue of books'. Maud Jeanne Franc is certainly not notable for a sense of irony, although there is plenty of fun and laughter in Matilda's stories. Still, it just possible that the name Franc, adopted for its connotations of frankness and truthfulness, gave Matilda a little extra pleasure as she tempered her hopefulness with a rueful view of possible failure.

CHAPTER 5

Happy in Such a Land

The chief charm of *Marian* today, and it was perhaps so even in its own time, is the freshness and enthusiasm with which Matilda has responded to the sights and sounds, the duties and experiences of this new world. *Marian* is a very positive, and in its quiet way even an enthusiastic, novel, and the view of country life given in it surely reflects the joy and wonder with which Matilda herself first made the acquaintance of a kind of life which was totally new to her. She may have been a struggling schoolteacher, rather than an eagerly awaited governess, but she had much in common with the heroine of her first novel. Both had to make a living, and both were prepared to like those amongst whom they had to work, and to love the place where the work took place. Matilda certainly loved the Mount Barker area. Her son Henry referred to her passion for it in an article on Mount Barker which he wrote in 1893 for the periodical *Quiz* of which he was editor.

> Mount Barker. Why, bless your simple heart, it's just one of the prettiest places in South Australia. You have read about it and its surroundings in the works of Maud Jeanne Franc, who used to live at Mt Barker in the early days, and who to the very last loved the place with an affection unspeakable.

At the time at which Matilda lived there Mount Barker was a prosperous agricultural district twenty-one miles (34 kilometres) south-east of Adelaide, by the roads then in existence, and Yunkunga was three miles (5 kilometres) further on. Travel to the area from Adelaide was by horse or dray or bullock wagon. The roads, little more than tracks, were dusty in summer and muddy in winter. It was a full day's journey from Crafer's Inn, at the top of the steep pull up from Adelaide to the hills, to Mount Barker.

The country was undulating with extremely fertile valleys and slopes, and small streams which ran most of the year, but the summits of the hills had little vegetation, and primary rocks of granite, quartz or sandstone were frequently exposed. The area was celebrated for its fine wheat—indeed Mount Barker wheat had won the prize medal at the 1851 London exhibition. Vegetation was luxurious and almost every house had a flourishing vegetable and flower garden. One of the most striking aspects of the world about which Matilda wrote was the vigorous growth of flowers and fruit trees in the gardens of the houses of her characters. All the settled areas of South Australia, including Adelaide, were rich in growth in those early days.

Matilda's heroine, Marian Herbert, is a confident and resolute young woman, who takes a position as a governess to Julie aged thirteen and Bessie aged eight on a 'farmstead' fifty miles from Adelaide, a fortnight after her arrival in the colony, because 'I want a home—I cannot stay with my friends; I wish to be useful and independent'. This was an attitude likely to meet with approval and understanding in the colony, as was the intention of Allen Burton, whom she was eventually to marry, to see that his sisters were well-educated. 'He knew that his sisters would have a handsome dower, and he longed to see them occupy a good position in the land of their birth. Education, he knew, was the first step on the ladder of life.'

Marian was kindly received by the Burtons, and she was not excluded from the family circle as happens so often in 'governess stories'. In fact once it was seen that she was a 'lady', that she was attractive to look at, and that she was full of charm and goodwill, she was positively embraced by the family, farmer Burton clearly hoping that she would marry one of his sons almost from the moment he saw her. It was a new departure in a governess story that marriage with the governess should be seen as a step in upward social mobility, especially as Marian is presented as completely lacking in any sense of social superiority. She accepted with pleasure that her duties included 'light domestic employment' and readily took part in many of the activities on the farm. It is worth pointing out that this is a very early governess story, even by English standards. According to Marion Amies in her study, 'The Victorian Governess and Colonial Ideals of Womanhood' (*Victorian Studies* Vol. 31, No. 4, 1988) it gives a fair picture of what governessing was like in colonial households.

Although Matilda's fictitious farmstead is fifty miles from Adelaide, the novel is set on a farm in the Yunkunga district, as any reader of the book who goes to the area even today can discover. Whether Matilda herself did the things which Marian did or whether she merely observed them we shall never know, but the enthusiasm which fills the early part of the novel suggests the enthusiasm with which she encountered what must have been a new world. Her heroine had always lived in London and 'was never even at a farm-house in England'. She was amused by the room—a bedroom, with packing-case furniture—specially put up to accommodate her, but Matilda shows that she was lucky in her situation.

> The rough, plastered, whitewashed walls, the calico ceiling, the uneven, loose-boarded floor, diverted her highly, and the quaint little window, in its wooden framework, unpainted, unpolished, seemed so strange to her. And yet in how many houses, instead of that calico ceiling, she would have looked up to the rafters, and seen the stars shining above her head; instead of that rough-boarded floor, her little feet, as she sprang from her bed, would have encountered the bare earth.
>
> *Marian*, p. 31

Marian adapted readily to the life, and accepted that although she was there to teach she herself had much to learn. Within a week she had begun to learn to milk, had churned and 'made up butter', sliced tobacco for Mr Burton's pipe, practised jumping her horse over a log, hunted for eggs with Bessie, and 'spoilt a beautifully crowned furrow' with Alf, a younger son, 'who insisted she should make a trial of the plough, because she told him "ploughing looked easy enough, though very awkward"'. She knew that she was there to work not play, however, and although occupied indoors with her two young pupils, teaching Julie among other things how to dress her hair as well as how to play the piano and how to love and depend on God, she entered fully into the life of the farm. At harvest time she rolled up her sleeves to make pastries for the lunch-bags of the workers, and even once when hands were short filled and refilled the tin dish for the winnowing machine while Alf turned the handle for the whole of one afternoon until she fainted with exhaustion. Allen, who hoped that she would eventually become his wife, found this occupation demeaning, but Marian herself merely remarked that she should have stopped sooner.

Convention may have found Marian's behaviour unsuitable, but to Matilda it appeared merely to be part of becoming adjusted to a new land, just as 'creeping under fences' when Marian and Julie took provisions to a sick labourer, was something necessary to be done, even though 'crinoline and muslin were never contemplated when the fence was made'. Women, not surprisingly, were given to fainting in novels written at that time. Marian was full of energy but her clothes were hardly suitable for farmwork.

I have said that Matilda was a conventional novelist, one who reflected rather than challenged the society in which she lived. Marian is in that way a conventional heroine: she had 'gentle blood' and brought with her 'relics of luxury', and her gentility shone through her conduct and self-control. Yet she had plenty of fun in her, and we can see in the way she adapted to colonial life and in the way she took part in activities such as ploughing a kind of behaviour which would have been staggeringly out-of-place in a 'genteel' governess in an English novel. The way she helped with menial tasks and her readiness to try a man's job—assisting at the winnowing—showed a different sort of governess, and reflected a new colonial freedom. In not merely accepting this freedom but effectively celebrating it Matilda did in effect actively challenge the class divisions with which she had grown up and helped to ensure that colonial society in South Australia would never be as dominated by class divisions as English society continued to be. Governess stories were always much read; it is not hard to see why this particular governess story became popular with English readers.

Matilda was very alive to the world around her, and one of the attractive things for a modern reader of *Marian* is seeing what this world was like to a newcomer. There are springs in the Yunkunga area, so that the creeks were always running, and Marian could look from her window and see a miniature cascade, and trees that she had not seen before.

> Grass, and huge blocks of rock, and flowers showing their blue heads, and trees—gold-tipped, light, feathery trees, new to her eye—the mystic she-oak, with its strange whispering leaves, in clusters they stood, here and there interspersed by an old gum or a young cherry tree.
>
> *Marian*, p. 32

Matilda very much loved the sheoaks; they are noted in many of her stories. But other trees, too, struck Marian's eyes: 'young wattles. . . yellow with profusion of blossom, and pouring their perfume on the early breeze', and blackwoods, and gums.

> The old gums—those gums upon which she had gazed so contemptuously when first she saw them after her voyage, comparing them with the gracefully timbered trees of Old England,—even they excited an interest—even they looked beautiful in the morning sunlight.
>
> p. 46

When she awoke on her first morning it was to the noises of farm life and to the new and frightening sound of the stockwhip:

> The lowing of cows, the cackling of hens, the neighing of horses, and the rumbling of the dray-wheels all burst upon her astonished ear together, and presently a strange, sharp, cracking noise without, followed by a rush of trampling hoofs, completed her consternation.
>
> p. 33

On an early morning walk on her first Sunday she was disturbed and a little frightened by what turned out to be the 'ridiculous laugh' of the 'singular bird', the 'laughing jackass'. But other sounds tell us more about Matilda's delighted response to Australian country life.

But now that merry triumphant laugh had swelled to a complete chorus, and at once the inmates of every nest responded. Some with sharp, shrill, single cries; some with strange twittering; some with a note or two sounding like the commencement of melodious bird-song, but no more than commencement; yet, above all—soft, clear, rippling, gushing—was poured forth the exquisite song of the native magpie, gurgling joyously; inexpressibly sweet and touching were some of the notes. It seemed as though that little throat throbbed with ecstasy.

p.48

At night the 'locust' sang its 'loudest notes of gladness', 'the bul-bul of the great bull-frog' sounded from the creek, and 'the more-pork sent forth its cuckoo-like note'.

Scents, too, Matilda seemed very aware of, both the well-known scents of violets and roses growing so lushly in newly-planted gardens and the new strange country scents of wattle and native flowers. In fact in most of her novels she so frequently comments on the native scents that I began to wonder if in an effort to impress possible English readers she was exaggerating. However, in the entry on Mount Barker in the 1867 edition of the *South Australian Gazetteer* comments about scents confirm the impression given by Matilda: 'Most of the uncleared land is covered with fine specimens of eucalyptus and acacia, beneath which flourishes a variety of orchids and other splendid flowering plants, many of them being delightfully fragrant.'

There are many references to native flowers in *Marian* and in her other novels, but particularly in *Marian* and *Vermont Vale* one is struck by the prevalence of the scarlet pea which we know as Running Postman (*Kennedia prostrata*). Bessie Burton goes 'flying through the room with a garland of wild scarlet pea-flowers wreathed round her slender figure'. These pea-flowers must have grown in great abundance. I have found them recently growing on the slopes of Mount Barker itself, and often plants can be seen in the scrub, but the way Matilda writes tells us of a time when they covered the ground in rich profusion. In *Vermont Vale*

Katie went laughing back in search of another scarlet wreath. She knew that if one was spoiled there were hundreds of the

> bright blossoms all over the sections through which her way lay; she could have covered herself entirely with them had she been so disposed. As it was, she contented herself with a wreath round her slight waist, and permitted the bright scarlet blossoms a hiding-place among her soft, sunny curls; for her hat was tossed to the ground as she twined her brilliant garlands.
>
> *Vermont Vale*, p. 22

Emily too refers to the 'scarlet Kennedya on the ground' in one of her Mount Barker poems.

The story of *Marian* is slight. Allen marries Marian. Julie dies of tuberculosis, the first of a number of characters who die of this disease with which Matilda seems very familiar. There are no mysteries, no discoveries, not even much depth of characterisation. The interest lies in the detailed and realistic picture of country life and in the gradual unfolding of the author's didactic purposes. The novel fulfils something of the function filled by women's magazines in my childhood and youth. There is advice to those who are not contented in this new world; women are shown how they might make their husbands' and their own lives more satisfying by turning their backs on the past and accepting their present lot, by decorating rooms tastefully, hanging new curtains, and paying attention to their clothes.

It is easy to laugh now at what appear to be superficial and banal solutions to the problems of immigrants. But Matilda had obviously observed and regretted the behaviour she describes, and believed that she had something positive to say to the local readers of her book. Isabel, the wife of Marian's cousin William, had to learn that slovenly behaviour, the result of her discontent with her new country, solved nothing. Isabel's problem was that she did not know how to fit into this new kind of community which was based on a new freer social order. Coming from a gentle background to an immigrant society where every household was a working household she was without initiative. She could not keep her house tidy. 'I was not brought up to it—I suppose that's it.' She and her husband are contrasting types, he energetic and ambitious, determined to make good, she backward-looking, longing to return to the past. This might well have been a common situation in colonial society.

> Alas! how seldom did she give him the opportunity for praise,
> not because she had ceased to care for his love—oh, no—but
> because she had grown careless and slovenly, dissatisfied with
> her home, adopted country, and everything around her.
>   Young wives, young wives! if you only knew how much love
> is cooled by this indifference to outward appearances!
>
> *Marian*, p. 216

There is something comical about unmarried Miss Congreve,
not much more than thirty years of age, laying down the law to
discontented immigrant wives, but the tone is consistent with the
personality of the narrator, Maud Jeanne Franc, and helps us to
understand why Matilda felt that she needed a pseudonym.

Her advice is incidentally not as conventional as it looks at
first sight. Certainly she stressed the need for wives to submit to
and please their husbands, yet in almost all her novels it is the
wives, not the husbands who have the real strength. And even in
Marian, when she was perhaps not yet so conscious of the strength
women needed to survive, she was well aware of the importance to
women's health of their attitude of mind. In the following passage
Isabel, who hates dusty Adelaide, is doing some soul searching,
having been awakened to the likely consequences of her negative
attitude by Marian.

> She was shaking a little of the dust from her mind. It had
> accumulated greatly since she had entered the colony.
> Necessarily it impeded her movements; the wings of her spirit
> were chained. She saw everything through a dust-cloud. All
> appeared to her gloomy. She had taken pleasure in nothing.
> Ought this state of things to continue? Young wife, for your
> husband's sake—*no*! Mother, for the sake of those little ones—
> thrice *no*! For the sake of your own health, mental and bodily—
> a thousand times *no*!
>
> p. 228

The progression is worth noting—husband first, then children,
then oneself. But the value placed on each is revealing—the
woman's own well-being is of first importance: not just no! but a
thousand times no! Matilda unmistakably was a woman with clear
and firm ideas about what was necessary to produce worthwhile
happy people. She believed that the colonists should make the

best of the world that they were in. In Marian's words, 'It is the fault of the discontented if they do not make themselves happy in such a land as this.'

Although this theme of advice to men and women, and particularly to women, is an important one, it is not the theme that she cared most about. Her greatest wish was to bring religion to those people in the colony who had strayed from its paths or perhaps had never known its blessings. Alf was quick to tell Marian that 'Sunday is not kept among the wattles'. Marian, by her constant witness and her gentle powers of persuasion, gradually induced the young characters in her story, Allen, Alf and Julie to take religion seriously. At first they merely set out to please her, but gradually all were changed by her influence. They rode with her the ten miles to the nearest chapel—'a little chapel, built of roughly hewn stone, and seated with plain benches'. One of their neighbours sneered at this chapel, calling its members 'Ranters'. Marian rebuked him saying they are

> Wesleyans, Mr Clare. They are a simple, earnest people, but I never heard of their ranting. I am not a Wesleyan, but I like some of the people very much. At any rate I think it pleasant to worship God in a house set apart for His service, when I have the opportunity.
>
> *Marian*, p. 147

There was in fact a Wesleyan chapel within walking distance of Yunkunga, and it seems likely that Matilda attended there before she moved to Mount Barker, and to the Presbyterian church. There was at that time no Baptist church in the area. Her readiness to accept what each of these denominations had to offer in her own life, and the use she made of her experiences in the novel, made her an approved novelist in a colony in which there was a large proportion of Dissenters and a general feeling that Godlessness was bad.

Conventional plots of romantic novels turn on the obstructions which keep hero and heroine apart until the last pages of the novel. *Marian* may be a conventional novel in some ways but the obstruction which kept the lovers apart is unusual. It was not forbidding parents—the Burtons are only too anxious for the union of Allen and Marian. It was not want of fortune or want of inclination. The lovers were kept apart because Marian would not marry unless her husband was able to make the same religious commitment that she had made. Merely sympathising or conforming would not do. She gave him her Bible, with the 'decisive words' underlined: 'Those that marry, let them marry in the Lord.' Allen knew he had a 'powerful rival', and he struggled for months before he was able to understand what her faith was and finally to share it.

This theme of absolute religious compatibility in marriage partners is found in several of Matilda's novels. It was something she cared deeply about. Yet when she was writing this novel she was a single woman, apparently without marriage prospects. The one photograph we have of her, taken when she was a prosperous woman of middle age, shows her to have been slender and perhaps delicate. She certainly does not look robust. She is attractive in appearance, with large striking eyes. She might, when young, have been very pretty. She looks quiet and unassuming, as all accounts of her insist that she was; nevertheless there is strength and firmness in her demeanour.

She must have thought about marriage, if not for herself— though that seems very unlikely—at least in so far as it concerned her novel. Perhaps she too had rejected a suitor who could not match the depth of her faith. Or perhaps observation had led her to see that such compatibility was essential when one partner was a committed Christian. In the struggling or unhappy marriages of her later novels always there is a partner who has no such commitment. It was a very real fear of Matilda and of characters in her novels that married lovers would be separated after death if one was an unbeliever.

> Think well of the consequences of wedding with one who, however tenderly loving and loved, cannot be yours for *eternity*. '*One* shall be taken and the other left.' One shall be taken and the other left. Oh! words of sad, of fearful import.
>
> *Emily's Choice*, p. 271

A similar fear made Emma Darwin, wife of Charles Darwin

whose *The Origin of Species* was published in the same year as *Marian*, deeply unhappy throughout what appeared otherwise to be an highly satisfactory marriage, and Charles the unbeliever was equally affected. This contemporary and well-documented example may help present-day readers understand the religious climate in which Matilda lived and wrote.

I think that hers was the kind of faith which frequently leads the believer to the ministry. Her novels are deliberate attempts to 'win souls for Christ' and sermons play no small part in them. If she had not been of the wrong sex she might well have been a preacher and pastor. As it was she did the best she could in her novels, and when it came to the question of her own marriage she chose a Baptist minister.

CHAPTER 6

Matilda's Choice

Ephraim Evans, who became Matilda's husband on 16 February 1860, had, like Matilda, known great sorrow and hardship. Not much is known of his early life nor of his first months in Australia. He too came from a religious background. He was born in Great Britain in 1825 of pious parents and was greatly affected by the sudden death of his mother from a stroke when he was twelve. His own sudden death suggests that he had inherited his mother's problem.

When he was nearly nineteen he became strongly conscious that he lived in a state of sin and it was some time before he was able to gain a sense of forgiveness and peace. In July 1846, at the age of twenty-one, he was baptised in the Borough Road Chapel in London and became a member of the church there. He was employed as a missionary in connection with the New Park-street Church. He worked with young people in the Sabbath and Ragged Schools and was instrumental himself in the establishment of a Ragged School at the New Cut. The school continued to flourish, well after its founder had left for Australia. He helped with money from Australia, and at the end of 1857, although his own income was still very uncertain, he sent a 'handsome donation of £4' to help with the work of the school.

In 1851 he married Mary Ann Wilton, a member of the church he belonged to, and in August or September 1852 his first son, named Ephraim for his father, was born. On 4 August 1853 the little family set sail in the *Leonidas* for Australia. They travelled either in the steerage or in the intermediate class, and arrived at Port Adelaide on 3 December. What Ephraim did when he first arrived in Adelaide I have not been able to discover, though he was soon to take steps to find a school. Before he had made that move, however, and while they were still living in the city, in Ebenezer Place in the East End off Rundle Street, disaster struck and their baby Ephraim, now sixteen months old, died of dysentery. This was a sad beginning to their life in South Australia.

Somehow or other Ephraim had heard that a schoolmaster was needed at Reedy Creek, near Tungkillo, not far from the present town of Mannum on the River Murray, where there were mines in operation and a school was needed for the children of the miners and of local farmers. In April 1854 the Board of Education received a letter from Mr Forster of Tungkillo Mine, asking for help in finding a schoolmaster—a Mr Steele had visited Tungkillo with a view to setting up a school. The Board replied, somewhat enigmatically, 'another person may soon visit Tungkillo with a view to commencing a school there whom the Board have reason to think would be found more eligible'. Evidently at least one member of the Board had had contact with Ephraim and was willing to recommend him.

The previous teacher at the Tungkillo Mine school had been John Martin, who was catechist for Bishop Short, the Anglican Bishop of Adelaide. Martin was a preacher as well as a teacher, and this is evidently what was needed in the district. By the beginning of May Mr Ephraim Evans had applied for the position and was found by Mr Forster 'to be better suited to the purpose'. Mr Evans however, both then and later, met with many problems during his career as a schoolmaster. To begin with he could not assemble a sufficient number of pupils to be considered for a licence, even though his school was at the time the only school in the Mount Pleasant area. At the end of June he had only fourteen pupils, but midway through July he could muster twenty-four and was then licensed from 1 July at the minimum stipend. He taught at the school during the week and preached on Sundays.

It seems likely that from the first his heart was not really in the teaching. He wanted to be, and would eventually become, a minister, and I imagine that it was in order to make possible preaching tours that he put in a very unusual request to the Board.

He asked leave 'as a matter of convenience to himself to take the month's holidays annually allowed by the Board in four instalments of a week each at the end of each quarter'. The Board endeavoured to be reasonable but asked that holidays not be taken at a time when the Inspector was due to visit. When almost a year later the Inspector found the school closed and the students on holidays when he arrived, the Board expressed some outrage and Mr Evans was required from that time on to keep to the regulation holidays.

His daughter Mary Ann—named after her mother but always called Pollie—was born at Reedy Creek on 12 February 1855, and in the next year on 17 April a second baby Ephraim, this time named Ebenezer Ephraim, was born. In the middle of 1856, shortly after Ebby's birth, Ephraim wrote to the Board resigning his licence at Tungkillo and requesting a licence for the school at Nuriootpa, which he intended to take over from another teacher who was moving. This was a public school supported by the residents of Nuriootpa. Dr Birks who had been the ship's doctor on the *Leonidas* was working at Angaston at this time and perhaps it was through him that Ephraim heard of the position. The Angas family were of course Baptists, and there was a growing Baptist community in the area. It seems at any rate that Ephraim believed he would have more scope for his ministry in the Barossa area.

Nuriootpa, previously known as Angas Park, was a small town in the Barossa Valley, a little west of Angaston and a little north of Tanunda. Its settlers were mostly German, but there were English farmers and vine-growers as well. I imagine that Ephraim was happier at Nuriootpa. It was not as isolated as Tungkillo, and in any case the future of the mines there was always uncertain. More importantly the Barossa area was at the time an area of great expansion for the Baptists, and Ephraim not only fitted in but became a leader in the spread of the Baptist faith. He must surely have been a dynamic preacher because in the next few years he is recorded as having preached at Lyndoch Valley, Sheoak Log, Nuriootpa, Angaston, Collingrove (the property of John Howard Angas), Tarrawatta, Flaxman's Valley, South Rhine, Salt Creek, Tungkillo and Gumeracha. He was active and very busy.

But without warning his life changed disastrously. On New Year's Day 1858 his wife died of pneumonia after a very short illness. He was still in charge of the Nuriootpa school but during the holidays he was working as a minister. He had gone out to visit the sick and had returned to find his wife dead. I do not know how he managed in the next two years. He must have made some arrangements for the two little children. Ebby was only nineteen months old when his mother died. It is an unlikely fancy that they went to Matilda for she must have been busy herself with her school and her writing and Emily was no longer with her.

Certainly Ephraim must now have found life very difficult with the children and the school, but whatever happened he refused to give up his preaching. In August 1859 things came to a head. The Board of Education received a letter from ten concerned citizens of the Nuriootpa area complaining that 'Mr Evans the teacher of the District School through having other engagements was not paying sufficient attention to his school duties' and that their children were not receiving a reasonable education.

The letter was forwarded by the Board to Ephraim who replied, enclosing a letter from a local inhabitant who did support him and a memorial from thirteen citizens who had confidence in him and wished to retain his services. The Board, though willing to support their licensed teacher, felt that Mr Evans must be to some extent responsible for the criticisms and for the small attendance at his school, and asked him to see that things improved. His opponents continued to bombard the Board with complaints, which Ephraim said stemmed from the fact that he was a teetotaller and recommended total abstinence. The young Barossa Valley wine industry was already well-established and in need of markets; in the circumstances it seems not at all unlikely that there should be a section of the Nuriootpa community antagonistic to a popular preacher who advocated total abstinence!

Ephraim must have known, however, that there was something in their charges of dereliction of duty because in October he wrote to the Board resigning his licence and from that time forward he devoted himself to pastoral duties. I suspect that though he now worked very hard indeed as pastor and preacher he very much missed the steady income which he had received as a schoolmaster. He had now no settled income, for country pastors were dependent for their livelihood on the generosity of those who made up their congregations. One gathers from Matilda's novels that such congregations responded readily enough to new and enthusiastic preachers, but these were such very small communities that it was only by much travelling and much hard work that a sufficient number of groups could be reached to enable the pastor to enjoy an adequate income. Nevertheless Ephraim took the risk and asked Matilda to share it with him.

Matilda had suggested in *Marian* that, though the visits to the nearest chapel were considered to be important, it was the place and the service, rather than the minister, which Marian valued. Just once, however, there was a visiting preacher, 'a young and gentlemanly looking man, whose brow, from which a profusion of dark hair was carelessly thrown, bore the impress of thought, and whose eye glowed with intellect and feeling'. This was a new kind of preacher who did not thunder from the pulpit but 'carried their hearts with him by his deep, rich voice, his persuasive tones, his affectionate exhortations'.

It is impossible now to know how Matilda and Ephraim met, but it is certainly not impossible that either at Mount Barker or elsewhere she heard a young dynamic preacher with whom she later agreed to share her life. They were married and he took her to live with him and his two little children at Nuriootpa.

The next three years were very busy ones, involving much travelling and absence from home. In 1861 for instance Ephraim travelled nearly 3,660 miles [5,856 kilometres] on horseback as he visited his various preaching stations, and held 231 services, that is at least nine services each fortnight, many of them no doubt on Sundays at different settlements separated by considerable distances. He also attended nine tea meetings, five trustee meetings, eight church meetings, spoke to three Bible classes and baptised six believers. Many of these services and meetings, of course, would not have been at Nuriootpa but at distant centres. Obviously this busy life would be a fulfilling one for the pastor, especially as his youthful enthusiasm was making its first impact on his audiences. He was completely dedicated to his work. 'As a Christian he enjoyed the religion he professed; it made him happy. Meet him when you may the smile was seldom from his face,' one of his friends wrote about him.

But for the young wife things were surely not easy. *Emily's Choice*, Matilda's novel about the married life of a struggling country minister, begins with a conversation between two older women who discuss the problems which are likely to beset Emily in her new situation. They do not dispute the love of the pastor and his wife for each other, but look realistically at what the wife's life will be like.

> She will have much to put up with—much to endure. Lonely days, and still more lonely evenings, will be her portion; grief on her own, and grief on her husband's account, at lukewarmness exhibited by his people in manner, and shortcomings in pocket. *Emily's Choice*, p. 3

This was the downside of his dedication, as Matilda knew by bitter experience when she wrote her novel after his death. It is clear from his many recorded absences that she must often have been lonely. It is hard not to assume that money worries also played a big part in their life together. In the preface to *Emily's Choice* Matilda wrote that she would believe it a 'high reward' for her efforts if through her book 'some zealous, hard-working country pastor' should experience 'greater consideration, kindlier treatment, and ungrudging payments from those whose duty it is to remember that "the labourer is worthy of his hire"'.

Added to money worries and loneliness was the responsibility of the children. Pollie, at the beginning of 1861 was nearly five and Ebby was three. Matilda's own first baby, Henry Congreve Evans, had been born at Nuriootpa on 10 December 1860. A fortnight later on Christmas Day Ephraim preached the first service in the new Salem Baptist chapel at Tungkillo, a little church some three or four kilometres south-east of the present town of Mount Pleasant. However much she supported him in his work Matilda must have have found this first Christmas as wife and mother to be a lonely one, for the Tungkillo church was nearly 50 kilometres from Nuriootpa, almost a day's ride.

By the end of 1861 Matilda was pregnant again. William James Evans was born on 17 June 1862. Matilda certainly had her hands full, and it is likely that loneliness and lack of money were not her only problems. The *Angaston and Nuriootpa Centenary Souvenir* booklet, published in 1936, tells us that during the early sixties the Aborigines at Nuriootpa were so troublesome that 'a stockade had to be built around the little homes'. Matilda did not use such incidents for her books. She wrote rarely of Aborigines and when she did she expressed merely a detached, perhaps slightly patronising, wonder and sympathy. Nevertheless, it cannot have been easy being often left alone in such a situation, sometimes only for the day and evening, but sometimes overnight, as Ephraim's duties took him further afield, or he was delayed by bad weather and bad roads or tracks.

Halfway through 1861, when Ephraim was away so much, leaving Matilda with the children, Emily resigned from the school at Prospect Village where she had been teaching since 1857. I have no information as to why she did this, but one possibility is that Matilda needed help and that Emily was prepared to supply it. A poem by E. C.[1], 'The Deserted Homestead' about a place near Tanunda, was published in *The Thursday Review* on 26 December 1861, and this suggests at least that Emily had been in the area. If this is what happened it seems that she may have remained with Matilda until after the birth of William on 17 June 1862.

But there were probably financial problems. Ephraim's income was always uncertain, if we can judge from the picture of a minister's life given in *Emily's Choice*, and maybe Emily could not be supported indefinitely in the Evans household even if she did provide much needed help. At any rate she returned to teaching from

1. E. C. was certainly Emily Congreve. There is a notebook of Emily's poems among the Congreve papers which contains poems published in *The Thursday Review*. See also Elaine Barker 'Who was "Little Jacob"?' in *Notes and Furphies* No. 32 October 1989. Obituaries published after Emily's death in 1896 make it clear that she was the author of *Colonial Pen-Scratchings*, although her nephew Henry Evans writing in *Quiz* mistakenly referred to her book as *Australian Pen-Scratchings*.

October 1862, taking up an established school at Athelstone, then a country village in the foothills northeast of Adelaide.

Like the Prospect Village school this was not in a flourishing area. The Inspector's report on the previous incumbent said that it was 'An elementary school, held in premises of limited accommodation and indifferently supplied with material. The attendance is fluctuating and irregular'. That Emily needed to take up this unpromising post suggests that they were in a difficult situation and that the money was important.

It is possible of course that she had not resigned from the Prospect Village School in order to go to help Matilda. It seems likely indeed that she suffered from illhealth all her life. A notebook in the possession of the Congreve family contains a poem of Emily's entitled 'Foreboding'. It was written in 1863 and ends with the words 'Live the time I have to live / In pain and gloom'. A postscript was added in 1884. 'Alas these Prognostications have proved only too true—20 years of pain and suffering.' In letters written much later Matilda speaks several times of Emily's ill-health. It may be then that Emily gave up the school at Prospect Village because she was not well enough to continue. If this was in fact the case it must have been another emotional and possibly financial burden upon Matilda.

Ephraim continued to be very busy in his church work, too busy, as it proved. When the new Baptist chapel on the Williamstown road near Lyndoch, at the south end of the Barossa Valley, was opened in January 1859, although he was then still the schoolmaster at Nuriootpa, he preached at the opening and became its first minister. In 1862, as there was help from some wealthy subscribers, including George Fife Angas who subsidised the church annually for some years, it was decided to sell that chapel—it is still there and now serves as a Lutheran church and day school—and to build a new chapel in the heart of Lyndoch town.

This chapel (which is also still standing, though with some additions) was opened on 31 August 1862 and Ephraim who was still the Lyndoch pastor preached at the morning service. He was one of the original trustees and was instrumental in setting up the Sunday school there. He had worked hard to assure the success of

this new church. But he still lived at Nuriootpa, some 17 kilometres away, a not inconsiderable distance to travel frequently on
horseback.

Ephraim's other big interests at the time were in areas equally
far from Nuriootpa, but on the other side of the Barossa Range.
He held services on alternate Sundays at Alexander Wishart's residence in Flaxman's Valley south of Angaston. Later a more central
location was found still further south at the home of pioneer
farmer Jacob Grigg at the South Rhine near Craneford. The
Baptist faith was making good progress in the area at this time and
when three people were baptised on 11 December 1859 it was
decided to establish the South Rhine Baptist Church.

It was at this time, when he was acting as pastor for both the
Lyndoch Valley and South Rhine congregations, that Ephraim
found himself forced to give up the school in Nuriootpa. It seems
extraordinary that he had managed both responsibilities for so
long. Land for a South Rhine Baptist Chapel on part of Section
512 was given by John Barraud and Ephraim laid the foundation
stone at an open air service on 19 November 1861. Reg Butler in
his history of the Mount Pleasant area *The Quiet Waters By* records
that after the service 'some 200 people sat down to high tea in a
specially-erected tent'. Angaston's Baptist preacher, the Reverend
John Hannay, who was married to George Fife Angas's daughter
Rosetta, announced that his father-in-law would donate £50
towards the building fund, providing the congregation matched
the amount. The congregation responded by donating £80.

Ephraim worked very hard for this new building just as he had
for the chapel at Lyndoch. At the same time he occasionally
helped with the Baptist community at Salt Creek, a district east of
Eden Valley, where a church had been formed in March 1861.
The Lyndoch church opened at the end of August 1862 and the
South Rhine chapel was to be opened at Easter 1863. In January
1863 Ephraim wrote to a gentleman who had helped to support
him in his work, giving him an idea of how he had been spending
his time, apart from his work for these two chapels. 'I forward
you a brief account of my efforts for the past twelve months:—
Travelled nearly 4,000 miles [6,400 kilometres], held 205 public

services, delivered 5 lectures, attended 8 tea meetings and baptized twice.' It is clear that he had worked unstintingly for his cause.

In March 1863, shortly before the opening of the South Rhine chapel, Ephraim and Matilda and the four children moved from Nuriootpa to a house adjoining the church. It was surely a move to make his life less strenuous, although the ride from the South Rhine to Lyndoch would be a demanding one.

Unfortunately the move was made too late. On Good Friday morning, the morning for the opening service of the chapel, on a beautiful autumn day, he left for the chapel after breakfast and family worship, but collapsed not far from his own home. He was carried home paralysed and unconscious, and remained in a semi-conscious state until his death on Easter Monday, 6 April 1863. The opening of the chapel went ahead as planned though the illness of their pastor cast a pervading gloom over the ceremony and celebrations, and the £13 collected that evening to help with the expenses of the building may well have been larger as a result of his distressing illness.

After a service in the Angaston chapel and a 'solemn address' by the Reverend J. Hannay, who delivered another short address at the graveside, Ephraim Evans was buried in the Angaston cemetery, close to the grave of his first wife. The little old cemetery established in 1847 on land bought from George Fife Angas for ten shillings and in use until 1869 can still be seen just off the main street. A board listing the plots shows Ann Evans in plot 65—the date of death given is the same as for Mary Ann—and Ephraim in plot 67.

The following Sunday a special memorial service was held in the chapel and at this service too Mr Hannay was the preacher. Both burial and memorial services were attended by unusually large congregations, many members of which had ridden long distances to be present. Newspaper accounts at the time say that Ephraim died at his home at the South Rhine, but both the death certificate and the Letters of Administration needed to wind up his estate (issued later by the probate office in 1879) called the area Flaxman's Valley.

He died of 'hemiplegia' or stroke. He was known to have

suffered from heart disease, and this was thought to have been aggravated by his 'arduous labours'. He had often ridden between 24 and 48 kilometres on Sundays, preaching three times at different stations. Obituary notices suggest that he was widely known, loved and respected, not only by the members of his own church, but by the public generally. Certainly he had been unremitting in his endeavours to spread the faith in which he believed.

The derelict little South Rhine Baptist church is still there today, a sad monument to Ephraim Evans's efforts and hopes. It stands, filled with hay, on the south side of Basil Roeslers Road, almost at the corner where it meets Craneford Road. The adjoining dwelling in which Ephraim and Matilda lived in happiness for such a short time—'about ten days'—has disappeared. Alongside the broken-down chapel is the grave of Hilton and George, the two young children of John Barraud who had given the land. They died in February of the next year, 1864.

Poor Matilda! For the second time sudden death had left her thrown on her own resources. Ephraim died intestate, and there were not even enough possessions to be disposed of at the time to demand Letters of Administration from the probate office. She was responsible for four little children, of whom the oldest had just turned eight and the youngest was nine months. The newspaper account, in an understatement, noted that the widow and four young children were 'not very well provided for'. A subscription was opened to help them and 'several gentlemen ... contributed liberally'.

I have spoken of the difficulties Matilda encountered, but there had clearly been much happiness too in their short married life. Matilda had continued writing, and early in her marriage had begun to contribute stories—especially stories for children—poems and sermon-like essays to *The Australian Evangelist*, a Baptist periodical published in Melbourne. That the first of these, 'Little Willie or the Early Called', which appeared in July 1861, was printed with the words 'Written for the Evangelist' suggests that Matilda had been asked to contribute.

Certainly between July 1861 and June 1866 she contributed constantly, writing among other things two full-length novels which were serialised. Her writings for this publication are carefully directed to an evangelical readership, and are much more concerned with teaching religious lessons and give a much narrower picture of religious life in the new colony than *Marian* had done. Throughout her writing life Matilda showed considerable skill in slanting her material to her market, a point to which I shall return later.

One story in particular is worth commenting on for the light it throws on her and her family. It differs from her other short stories of the time in being told for itself, rather than for its lesson, though of course a lesson is drawn from it. What is special about it is that it uses the names of Polly, Ebby and baby Harry and that it appears to be drawn from the life of the family. 'Ebby's Hen' appeared on the children's page of the *Evangelist* on 21 March 1863. It gives just a glimpse of a stable and happy family life, the only glimpse we have. It suggests as well Matilda's comfortable relationship with her stepchildren.

Polly, ' a little girl about eight years old with light brown hair and rosy cheeks', baby Harry, 'her little dark eyed, auburn curled brother', and Mamma were awaiting the arrival of Papa and Ebby after a day or two away. Ebby when he arrived was very excited.

> 'Polly!' shouted her brother from the cart, 'I've got a fowl; its only *mine*. Mrs W—— gave it to me.'

He had been given an ugly-looking chicken which he named Jessie after a favourite little girl. The children eagerly waited for the chicken to grow up and the first egg to arrive.

> When do you think my fowl will lay, mamma?' was the eager exclamation one fine day, some time after it had been domesticated among its fellows.
>
> 'Ah; it will not be very long I dare say,' said mamma. 'You must watch it to see where it makes a nest.'
>
> 'I think it will not be very long either. I drove it to-day, and it made a noise like laying,' replied Ebby gravely.
>
> So poor Jessie was every now and then driven round the yard; and when in her terror she uttered her peculiar cackling noise, Ebby hoped for *eggs*!

Finally of course the hen did lay; the excitement engulfed the whole family. The eggs were examined, treasured, dropped, and even once crushed by 'the mischief-loving little fingers' of baby Harry. Ebby was delighted with Jessie.

> Ebby was very proud of his hen, and would have taken her in his arms and caressed her; but she was rather shy of caresses, and viewed every attempt at a capture as a decided hostile attack.

Then Jessie gave up laying and moulted. Ebby resorted to the 'driving process' again. This produced cackling but no eggs. Ebby was so angry he wished he had no fowl, and was ready to give her away. And so Maud Jeanne Franc could draw a moral of ingratitude. It is a very mild, pedestrian little story, but it is valuable in the one happy glimpse it gives of Matilda's married life, of children leading lives full of freedom, of fun, and of curiosity. It was obviously written to amuse them all, and it seems especially sad that it is unlikely that their copy had arrived from Melbourne before Ephraim's death. One hopes that they had as a family shared and laughed over this little tale.

Unfortunately such happiness was now over, at least for the time being. Matilda had once again to set out to rebuild her life.

CHAPTER 7

There Was But One Thing to be Done

No doubt Matilda had many good friends among the congregations with which her husband had worked. She would have needed them, while she worked out how she could support herself and the four little children. Obviously she could not stay at the South Rhine. If the only thing to be done was to open a school, then she must go to a centre where there was a big enough population to draw sufficient numbers of students.

She could not once again become a licensed teacher because the responsibility of the four little children would make such a commitment too risky—Willie was not yet a year old. She could hardly ask Emily to give up her school to come to help because with four children to support on a licensed teacher's stipend she would be unlikely to be able to support another adult. In any case the Board of Education would not license a teacher if there was already a school in the area whose existence might be jeopardised by the new licence.

There were two big Board of Education schools in the nearest large town, which was Angaston, and luckily for Matilda one of them was about to become a school for boys only. Edward Nesbit's well-established school had previously been a mixed school for boys and girls, for both boarders and day pupils. In 1864 Nesbit changed to a school for boys only. Richard Thomas's school had twenty-seven boys and forty-one girls, but Nesbit's boys' school had over fifty boys, so that there appeared to be an opportunity for an independent Young Ladies' Establishment.

Clearly then the best thing to do would be to move to Angaston and open a boarding school for girls. By the beginning of 1864 she had done this, for it was from there that she wrote an obituary for a former friend, Mary Ellen Wansbrough, who had died at the end of December 1863 at the South Rhine. She must have at first been in lodgings, for her name does not appear in the 1865 Adelaide Almanack which listed the names of ratepayers in South Australia for the previous year. But by the end of 1864 she was established in her new school.

On 5 September 1864, Emily resigned from the Athelstone school, and she did not again take up a position with the Board of Education. It is natural to assume that she now returned to live with Matilda, who had a home and a job for her. Probably from now on the sisters were frequently though not always together until Matilda's death. In 1865, according to the 1866 Adelaide Almanack, Mrs Evans was listed as a schoolmistress in Angaston, and during that year her three boys attended the Baptist Sunday School there. Ebby and Harry, at that time aged nine and five, attended throughout the year, although in different classes. From October little Willie (who was just over three) went too, and sat in Harry's class.

The Angaston District Council records are not available earlier than 1868, but they reveal that in the year which ended in June 1868 Matilda was renting two properties on section 331, a house and garden at an annual value of £22 and a schoolhouse and garden at an annual value of £12. She was in arrears, which tells us something of her financial struggles, but had paid the money owing by the end of 1868.

Section 331 includes the present Recreation Park and Council Chambers in Angaston so that it is clear that Matilda had a good central location for her school, and was reasonably successful, in spite of the amount of competition at the time. Her school was situated at what is now 9 and 11 French Street. The long, low, substantial house at 9 French Street is still standing. It is an attractive house but would have needed to be stretched to find accommodation for the boarders. In April 1867 an advertisement in *The South Australian Temperance Herald*, in which her novel *Minnie's Mission* was being serialised, reveals that 'Mrs Evans receives nine Young Ladies to Board and Educate, and has a vacancy for three.

Prepayment, quarterly on entrance'. It is my presumption that she would also have taken fee-paying day pupils, for this was current practice, and the records tell us that one of her houses was used as a school-house. The fees which were charged by licensed teachers were between fourpence and one shilling per week, and there seems to be no reason why Matilda could not have charged that or more.

Angaston was a comparatively wealthy area, and there were certainly rich people living on properties nearby. George Fife Angas and his descendants were Baptists, as were many of his friends, and although most had private tutors or schools on their properties some of them could well have been interested in a Baptist teacher for their daughters. Matilda certainly had some connection with the Angas family, not only through the contributions of George Fife Angas to her husband's work, and the association with the Reverend J. Hannay who conducted Ephraim's funeral service, but also through the illustrations which George French Angas did for *Vermont Vale* and *Emily's Choice*, and probably also through an acquaintance with George Fife Angas's second daughter, Sarah Lindsay Evans, who like Matilda was a staunch supporter of the temperance movement.

Matilda said later in *Beatrice Melton's Discipline* that there was nothing for an educated woman to do in circumstances such as hers except teach, and probably that was the only way in which she could be assured of a regular income. But in Angaston, as she had done in Mount Barker and Nuriootpa, once she was settled she began to write.

The 1860s proved an extremely productive period for her. *Vermont Vale; or Home Pictures in Australia* began to appear in *The Australian Evangelist* in August 1863 and continued in fortnightly episodes until July 1864. This must have been promised and partly written, if not already completed and sent, before Ephraim's death. In those very difficult months when she was grief stricken and preoccupied with planning for the future she could surely not have had a sufficiently uncluttered mind to begin a new story. It may however have been necessary to finish one already begun in this troubled time. Certainly *Vermont Vale* is a sober story and it does seem to lose some vigour towards the end. But the opening chapter, with its picture of the 'little unpretending Sabbath-house' in 'almost the prettiest place in the vale', and of its bachelor pastor clearly in need of a wife, suggests that Matilda at least began the book in compliment to her husband, and that it was intended to end in happiness as it had begun. That things went wrong was not to have been expected. The conclusion is in tune with Matilda's usual view of life, but there is something in some of the wording which suggests that she has had to come to terms with personal sorrow.

> Our task is done; we have longed for your souls, dear young friends; we have anxiously sought to induce you to love the Saviour whom we love. Ah! and why are we so anxious? Because this world is a fleeting dream at best—the reality is beyond! Because all here is passing away; because earthly joys are delusive, earthly hopes unstable, and nothing out of Christ worthy our confidence.
>
> *Vermont Vale*, p. 388

The story is set in a tiny country town in an area not unlike that surrounding Angaston. The frontispiece to the 1866 English edition, by George French Angas, shows a little town very like that in the famous painting of German Town, Angaston, which had appeared some years earlier in *South Australia Illustrated*. Angas lived just out of Angaston at his brother's house 'Collingrove' from 1860 to the beginning of 1863, when he returned to England for good.

While in Angaston he gave lectures on his travels. Perhaps it was through these or perhaps it was through the Baptist church that he met Matilda. He must have known her. That he should have provided the frontispieces for the English editions of *Vermont Vale* and *Emily's Choice*, published in 1866 and 1867 respectively, when he was permanently resident in England, would otherwise be inconceivable, for he is not known to have done other work of this kind.

The illustration to *Vermont Vale* is unsigned but the author of the review in *The Register* tells us that it was 'drawn expressly for the work' by George French Angas. The illustration to *Emily's*

Choice, which shows Emily at the door of their cottage farewelling her pastor husband as he rides off to his distant preaching station, bears the initials 'G.F.A.'. The book was later advertised in Sampson Low's catalogues as having a frontispiece by George French Angas.

The little village of Vermont Vale was perhaps more like the small settlements of Nuriootpa or Flaxman's Valley than it was like the flourishing town of Angaston. The chapel with the minister's house adjoining, the little house of the schoolmistress with its schoolroom attached, the doctor's house, the general store and a few farms—these made up Vermont Vale. The area as Matilda describes it could not possibly have provided the number of pupils that attended the large schools in Angaston. The heroine of the story is Katie Linwood, the bright active laughing young sister of a farmer in the Vale, who comes to keep his house, who is not a Christian and who must learn to accept Christianity before she is worthy of marriage to the pastor.

Vermont Vale was extensively and respectfully reviewed in South Australia when it appeared in book form in 1866, having been published in London by Sampson Low. But it was generally thought to be inferior to *Marian*. Her critics did not all approve of her narrow views. It was thought extreme to condemn all dancing on principle, as the stern Maud Jeanne Franc had done, and most reviewers disapproved of the way she constantly held up her story to preach.

There is no indication that any of her reviewers knew that the work had been brought out some years before in a Melbourne evangelical journal. If they had they might have appreciated the skill with which Matilda had slanted her material to suit her audience. All the stories Matilda wrote for the *Evangelist*, with the exception of the uncharacteristic 'Ebby's Hen', have the same rather heavy preaching style and the same fervent didacticism.

> And ah! if but one of our dear readers—if but one discovers through the medium of these few poor pages the emptiness of the world, and preciousness of Jesus—if but one is brought, like Katie, to sit at the Saviour's feet, our desire will indeed be accomplished; for we feel indeed

'Tis worth a world of shame and loss,
To draw one sinner to the cross.'

Vermont Vale, p. 388

This style continued in her next novel, but it is not found in later novels which were addressed to a very different readership and which were not subject to Ephraim's influence. *Vermont Vale* was not unappreciated though. Most reviewers found much to praise, particularly its realistic picture of Australian life 'which none but one who has lived in the country not far from Adelaide could have written'.

Emily's Choice when it first appeared in *The Australian Evangelist* between July 1865 and June 1866 was called '*Joys and Sorrows*', *An Australian Tale*. Every episode was preceded by the verse

Oh! tis not in grief to harm me,
While Thy love is left to me;
Oh! 'twere not in joy to charm me,
Were that joy unblest by Thee

It is, for all its name, a peculiarly joyless novel, as is indeed indicated by the little verse. It suggests that Matilda had a hard struggle to come to terms with Ephraim's death, and that she was only too aware that the many difficulties associated with the life of a country pastor had contributed to it.

The story deals with the early married life of Gilbert, like Ephraim a struggling country minister, and gently born and very gentle Emily his wife. Gilbert is shown as a dedicated minister who worked very hard, riding many miles in heat and rain to fulfil his ministry, grooming his own horse, and suffering deeply because his congregations were fitful and grudging in their response, often not keeping to their contract to support him with a stipend. The trials were many. Money became so short that gentle inexperienced Emily, who had no liking for teaching, was forced to take on the village girls' school, while Gilbert worked increasingly hard until he was subject to headaches and other aches and pains and was clearly on the edge of a breakdown. The seemingly frail and gentle Emily, already the mother of one child and pregnant with the next, arranged with her affluent brother for Gilbert to be sent on a mission to Melbourne to give him a sea voyage and time to recover. He came back refreshed in every way, having found a new congregation in Victoria which was prepared to welcome them both and support them in financial comfort.

In his absence Emily, worn out with her efforts and drained of all energy by being constantly at the bedside and later deathbed of a young consumptive whom she had converted to God, gave birth to a baby which did not live. This terrible sorrow seemed not to impinge upon Gilbert who was happy to be reunited with Emily and to feel himself the means of leading her to better circumstances. Gilbert is always a shadowy figure, a character whom the narrator esteems but dares not regard steadily, or examine.

This novel must in some ways mirror the difficulties which Ephraim and Matilda had experienced. Of course it is fiction, but she clearly wrote from knowledge of a pastor's life. It is interesting to us today partly because it shows the woman proving to be the stronger character, although she herself is not aware of this, and I am not even sure that Matilda was aware of what she was showing.

She was a survivor herself and her female characters tend to have the qualities of endurance and persistence necessary to survival. She was desirous of presenting her pastor as ideal, despite the fact that he was having difficulties with his congregation and was to some extent selfish and self-centred in his relationship with his young wife.

The story has value because it gives such a vivid picture of the trials in the life of the pastor and his wife, but the sketchy, unsatisfying and unsatisfactory conclusion also suggests that Matilda had some trouble in coming to terms with the fact that her fictional pastor could recover and overcome his problems while her own husband had not survived, and because of this had in a sense failed her. Yet in spite of its sombre nature *Emily's Choice* was always one of the most popular of Matilda's books.

Ephraim's influence had certainly sobered Matilda. *Marian* had been essentially a happy, expansive book in spite of its author's dissenting beliefs and earnest intentions. The greater narrowness and rigidity of the views put forward in *Vermont Vale* cannot be completely explained by its having been written for a different readership.

Nor can the joylessness of *Emily's Choice* be completely explained by Ephraim's death. 'The Forgotten Resting Place', a story published in *The Australian Evangelist* in June 1863 and which must have been written before her husband's death, gives another indication that Matilda had learnt extreme views from him. In this story Fanny Hampdon, although she had been 'a Christian bride', had allowed herself to love her baby with a love that was more than idolatry. When the child became ill she was unable to trust God and believed He had forsaken her. The narrator suggests that God was deliberately taking away her baby in order to remind her of His love. 'Yet God was only reminding her of her forgotten resting place; each touch was a touch of love, only love!' The baby died, though Fanny lived long enough to be reconciled to God.

There is a horrifying aspect to this view of God and a lack of real compassion in the telling of the story. There is no other of Matilda's surviving writings which is as narrow and unpleasant. After Ephraim died and Matilda had dealt with the pain in *Emily's Choice*, she returned again to writing in her former cheerful positive manner. *Minnie's Mission* and *Golden Gifts*, the two novels which followed, show a kinder more charitable God and are full of enthusiasm for living.

Much of the dismissive criticism of Matilda's novels has come from readers who have concentrated on *Vermont Vale* and *Emily's Choice*. It was the appearance of *Emily's Choice* in 1867 which prompted Eustace Mitford's virulent attack on the 'Vermont-Vale School' in his witty and influential weekly review *Pasquin: Pastoral, Mineral, and Agricultural Advocate*.

Four months after *Joys and Sorrows* concluded in the *Evangelist* in June 1866, *Minnie's Mission, An Australian Temperance Tale* began to appear in the new periodical, *The South Australian Temperance Herald*. It was announced in the August number as 'An Australian Temperance Tale, written expressly for our pages, by the popular authoress of "Marian" and other works'. It ran until April 1870 in the *Temperance Herald*, but it had been published in London in 1869 and was already available in Adelaide in book form by August of 1869.

Perhaps the editors of the *Temperance Herald* were attracted to Matilda by her handling of the temperance issue in *Vermont Vale*, in which Katie's brother Stephen was seduced by the colonial wine then becoming so popular in the area, and after several bouts of drunkenness fell off his horse, broke both his legs and died from the effects of his excesses.

This however was a small part of the story. In *Minnie's Mission* Minnie's efforts to persuade her uncle and cousins to take the pledge are central. One does not have to agree with Matilda on this point of 'temperance' to see that she has handled the matter with some skill and honesty. Her drunkards are not lower class and uneducated labourers, typed by their weaknesses, but the wealthy, well-intentioned, good-hearted farmer and his sons who when inebriated terrorised and physically mistreated the women of the household.

These are not the only alcoholics in the story. It is Minnie's mission to discover as many as she can and to persuade them to reform. She has considerable success, but she pays with her life, as she catches cold after descending to the cellar in the depths of the night, breaking all the wine bottles and emptying the barrels and kegs in order to make it impossible for her cousin Harry to imbibe. The story is nicely calculated to please its intended audience. In spite of its serious subject and its melodramatic ending it is in many ways a cheerful entertaining story which contains much fun and laughter.

Minnie's Mission was the first of four temperance novels, and one longish story on the same theme. It had not been an issue in *Marian*. It was not until she married Ephraim that the theme of temperance entered Matilda's novels. Ephraim was active in the temperance movement, both in Nuriootpa where he had clashed with local inhabitants and in Angaston. *The Register* reported that on New Year's Day 1861 at a public meeting of the Angaston and Penrice Total Abstinence Society the Reverend Ephraim Evans gave a highly interesting address.

Matilda was still living at Nuriootpa at that time, but she had obviously learnt to share Ephraim's beliefs. In *Vermont Vale* and *Emily's Choice* all drinking of wine and spirits is presented as evil, dangerous and incompatible with Christianity, but even though the readers of the *Evangelist* would have been sympathetic to attacks on drinking the theme is still peripheral to the main issues. It seems likely that Matilda became actively involved in the temperance movement when she came to live in Angaston after Ephraim's death and was persuaded then to begin to write temperance novels.

The movement was very strong in Angaston, fears having been aroused by problems associated with the growing wine industry. Many of the great landowners like George Fife Angas and his son John Howard Angas were growing vines on their properties. Henry Evans, husband of Sarah Angas, George Fife's second daughter, a close friend of the Angas family, had in 1852 planted the earliest vines in the Keyneton district at his home Evandale, a few miles east of Angaston, had produced a considerable amount of superior wine, had had great success with exporting, and had built what was believed to be the biggest winery in the colony.

All these men took their public duties seriously, but sometimes their private lives did not fit comfortably with their public lives. As local aristocrats they belonged to a class which drank wine with meals, but they were also members of strict religious groups. They built chapels on their properties for the benefit of themselves and their employees—as did also Joseph Gilbert not far away at Pewsey Vale—and the wine they produced was of good quality and unadulterated.

Abuse of alcohol however soon came to be a problem in wine-growing areas in a way that is hard for us to understand without special knowledge. The Australian wines which we drink now usually have an alcoholic content of between 11% and 14%. At the time of which I am writing the wines which the agricultural and other labourers drank often had an alcoholic content of 26% or even 30%. This was a mixture of new wine and added spirit, sometimes brandy, sometimes raw potato whisky. Many small farmers grew their own vines, and without skill in winemaking produced an adulterated beverage which was very nearly poison.

Even some of the better wines were much stronger than drinkers had been used to in other countries. Anthony Trollope visiting South Australia in 1872 had hard things to say about the local wines. He was afraid that a second or third glass would make him 'tipsy' which was not what he was used to! He thought South Australian wines had a 'heaviness about them' which made him afraid of them and pointed out that publicans could sell this wine at 2d. a glass.

Alcoholism had become such a problem that by 1874 a group of public spirited men began the movement which resulted in the creation of an Inebriate Asylum. The inaugural meeting was chaired by John Howard Angas who said in his address that alcoholism was a 'matter which affected, directly or indirectly, almost, if not every family in South Australia: indeed he believed there were few families who had not some branch or other addicted to the vice of intemperance.' He added that the high wages which could be earned in Australia had induced men to drink more.

It was in this context that Matilda began writing temperance novels. She knew people in the Angaston temperance movement and responded to their concerns. Sarah Evans, although her husband had a significant wine-growing business, was at least from 1859 a staunch supporter of the temperance movement and attended temperance meetings in Angaston and Keyneton. She believed that winemaking encouraged intemperance.

When her husband died suddenly in 1868, (while *Minnie's Mission* was appearing in *The South Australian Temperance Herald* and while Matilda was still living in Angaston), Sarah took immediate action. She had the cellars emptied, the vines either uprooted and destroyed or grafted for currants. The areas were replanted with fruit trees and the Temperance meetings were now held in the empty cellars. Later Sarah presided over the building of a Temperance Meeting Hall in Keyneton, for which she gave the land and a considerable sum of money. Her father George Fife and her brother John Howard Angas also contributed. By 1883 Sarah had sponsored the building of a Temperance Hotel at Keyneton and she later became a founding member of the Woman's Christian Temperance Union.

Though I have been unable to establish that Matilda was a member of the Angaston Band of Hope and Total Abstinence Society, to which Sarah belonged until the Keyneton branch was formed in 1870, it seems highly likely. Her novels show her to have been familiar with the language used by members of the temperance movement and a number of them deal with the 'signing of the pledge'. It is not surprising that she was asked to write temperance novels.

Hall's Vineyard, which was published in 1875, was written at the request of some of the leading citizens of Angaston who believed that wine was proving too much of a temptation to young people—so Matilda's brother Henry's daughter, another Emily Congreve, told the Reverend W. Gray in 1930. Sarah Evans was surely one of those citizens. Matilda was considered a very successful writer of temperance stories. One of them—unfortunately I have been unable to discover which one—was awarded a prize offered by the Scottish Temperance Society for the best novel dealing with the 'liquor question'.

The second novel of this period—a very different kind of novel for a very different audience—was appearing at the same time as *Minnie's Mission*. On 17 May 1867 *The Kapunda Herald*, a flourishing country newspaper, carried the message:

Notice to the Public:
A new serial tale by the author of 'Vermont Vale', 'Emily's Choice' etc, written expressly for this journal , and entitled 'Golden Gifts', will be commenced in our next issue.'

This was not the first novel by a member of the family to appear in *The Kapunda Herald*. Emily Congreve, using her former synonym of 'Little Jacob', had published a serial *Floy; A Tale* which ran from 5 October 1866 to 15 March 1867. It is an extravagant and sensational novel which has little to recommend it, but it is interesting in making it clear that sometime after she gave up the school at Athelstone Emily went to visit her brother Henry at Inglewood in Victoria. Henry married Jane Marshall Kirkwood, formerly of Glasgow, in Inglewood on 14 December 1865. William Congreve attended the wedding and it seems likely that

Emily did too. *Floy* is set in Inglewood and the detailed descriptions of the landscape and the goldfields make it certain that Emily had been there. When Matilda came to write a novel partly set in the goldfields there is no such detail or immediacy of description. It saddens me to think that Matilda was unable to join the others for the wedding, but I fear it was so.

Golden Gifts ran from May 1867 until March 1868, and in October 1869 was issued in Kapunda in book form. The publishers, Scandrett and Elliott of *The Kapunda Herald*, had obviously always intended to do this for the typesetting done for the newspaper was made to fit the page size for book publication. Three columns were made two. This looks very odd in the newspaper, but it facilitated the transition to book form. (*Floy* was not printed in this way.)

Golden Gifts must have sold well, for a second edition was brought out by E. S. Wigg, a well-known Adelaide Baptist bookseller and publisher, in Adelaide in 1874. For the next dozen or so years E. S. Wigg regularly advertised that he had all the novels of Maud Jeanne Franc in stock. Surprisingly, since it is such an attractive pioneering tale, *Golden Gifts* was not published in England until 1883. This may have been because it remained in print in South Australia, and the local publishers objected. It seems more likely that Scandrett and Elliott lacked expertise as publishers, for the fact that *Golden Gifts* is the only one of Matilda's novels for which I have been unable to find reviews in the South Australian papers suggests that they did not send out review copies. It may be that Matilda got less return from this novel than she might have hoped for.

Golden Gifts is one of the most attractive of Matilda's novels, and it too is a story written to attract a particular audience, the readers of a big farming area. This time it is a story of pioneer settlers, who settled not far from the Mount Barker road, in the Mount Lofty Ranges east of the area known at the time as The Tiers. Martin Wallace and his young brother Harry built their own slab hut and farmed their own land. Martin became a successful market gardener, using the skills he learned as a hobby when he lived in comfort in England. Until they could afford a servant his gently brought-up sisters took part in the rough work of the farm, even doing the heavy washing, which seemed to them the worst of their tasks. Nevertheless when the job was done they felt a real sense of pleasure and satisfaction 'in spite of aching backs, and weary feet, and terribly blistered hands and arms'.

At the close of the novel all their efforts were destroyed when a bush fire swept through their property. Luckily some news from England resurrected their fortunes. It is a pioneering story for a hardworking pioneering community, and although the characters are devout Christians, whose God is never far from their thoughts, and whose influence and example convert others to Christianity, there is little preaching.

The writer who reviewed *Vermont Vale* for *The Register* had added the comment that 'She should put a blacky or two in her next work, and describe them as they really are'. This was in September 1866. Matilda was probably already writing *Golden Gifts* when she read this review. Several pages early in the novel describing a group of aboriginals appear to be a direct response to this request, and suggest that though Matilda had seen and carefully observed aboriginal people she had known none personally. They are described as curiosities rather than as people. They were 'picturesque' at a distance but frightened Edith, who had never seen 'natives' before, when they came close.

> She turned and glanced to the window, and gave a startled spring to her brother's side; for peering through the glass were two pairs of very black eyes, rendered more conspicuous still by the whiteness of the eyeballs; two shaggy heads of hair; and two mouths of very white teeth, stretched to their widest extent by the sudden panic they had occasioned ...
>
> It was a woman, wrapped in the customary dirty blanket; and from behind her shoulders, enfolded in another, depended a tiny piccaninny, more than half white, with a head covered by lovely auburn curls—for lovely they were, even amidst the dirty surroundings—and dark eyes, that glistened and gleamed with curiosity and cunning, that strangely befitted such a tiny face.
>
> *Golden Gifts*, p. 59

The black people aroused amusement in Edith and anger in

Harry; nevertheless they gave them food clothes and money. There is just a suggestion that the author could see more clearly than her characters. When Harry asked the boy where he came from, ' "River Murray" was the curt reply, with a twinkle of the grave-looking black eyes'. The little scene is not to our taste today and Harry's impatience and dismissive attitude is particularly offensive. Edith however is shown as thinking seriously, if ineffectually, about the matter.

> 'And then to think that these beings are really of one blood with us!' replied replied Edith. 'Does it not seem strange? They have souls; and yet how near they seem to approach the lowest order of animals! I wonder whether there is really any effort made to do them good?'
>
> *Golden Gifts*, p. 61

It seems unlikely that this passage was written especially for the English market as apparently no effort was made to publish the book in England for many years. The fact that the incident has no bearing on the story at all and that aboriginal people do not appear again as characters in any of her stories suggests to me that this was indeed a response to the reviewer's request and that this in fact was all she could do because it was all she knew. Her brother Henry, however, who had lived with aboriginal people at Port Lincoln and had encountered them elsewhere in Australia, wrote many stories and sketches with aboriginal characters. For his time he showed little prejudice, taking blacks and whites as he found them, and often showing liking and respect for blacks as well as whites.

By 1869 Matilda was an established novelist—yet a comment in *Golden Gifts* suggests that it was at great personal cost. She speaks of the glass of flowers she has before her as she writes at which she occasionally glances 'to obliterate from memory the hard school-desk' upon which she 'pens down' her thoughts. There is no reason to doubt this authorial comment and it suggests, to me at least, that Matilda did not write in leisure and comfort, but that she had to set her self apart and write when and where she could. Certainly at this point in her life she must have written constantly and with great perseverance.

Her work was now accepted both in South Australia and overseas, but however successful she might have appeared to be her situation was still precarious. The evidence is scarce but the rather unhappy story of her stepchildren suggests that the difficulties were substantial. The responsibility and the expense of the stepchildren were beginning to tell. Pollie was now thirteen and Ebby was eleven. Pollie had been educated in Matilda's school, but some provision must now be made for her future.

With the help of George Fife Angas negotiations were entered into with some of the children's relatives in England, and at the end of 1868 they were sent to Ephraim's stepmother. As it turned out they were not wanted, were not well-treated and were unhappy in England, but they remained there until they were old enough to fend for themselves. Ebenezer entered the employment of J.B. Maple & Co., but ill health and unhappiness made Australia seem an attractive prospect.

When Pollie was twenty-three, in 1878, they returned to South Australia where they settled in the north at Tarcowie, Ebenezer in charge of the store there and Pollie as his housekeeper. Pollie taught music in the district and in 1882 married a local farmer, Joseph Lines. They had eight children. Pollie did not lose touch with Matilda. She brought her first child Lilian to see Matilda in North Adelaide in 1885. Pollie, who lived until 1937, has many present day descendants.

Ebenezer married Rachel Drake of North Adelaide in 1881. A son Leonard Wilton was born on 26 November 1882 while Ebenezer was still the storekeeper at Tarcowie. Later the family went to Fremantle in Western Australia, where Ebenezer kept a store for a number of years.

When the two stepchildren had left for England, and she was faced with the necessity of giving her own two boys a suitable education, Matilda took the last big step of her life. With Emily, Harry and Willie, now aged eight and six, she moved to Adelaide to set up a school there.

CHAPTER 8

Angaston House Establishment

It was on 6 March 1869 that the first advertisement for Matilda's new school appeared. Obviously she had not moved to North Adelaide much before this, for the preface to *Golden Gifts* which appeared in book form later in the year carries the subscript 'Angaston, March, 1869'.

The new school was first advertised as Angaston-Cottage, but the name was changed to Angaston House within a few days. Judging from the fact that the rateable value of the house, or house and school as it was later described, was only £32 it must have been fairly small. The term 'cottage' was probably appropriate, but not prudent, which accounts for the sudden change in name. It was on the south side of Buxton Street and on the third section west of Jeffcott Street. The advertisement spoke highly of the site. 'The house is situated in one of the most pleasant and healthy parts of North Adelaide, a short distance beyond Wellington Square'. It was to be 'an Institution for Young Ladies' conducted by Mrs E. Evans and 'competent masters'. The school was to open on 15 March which was more than half way through the first quarter, and since the advertisement occurred only one week before the opening, we must assume that Mrs Evans had already made arrangements with a number of pupils.

The advertisement informs us that Mrs Evans, recently from Angaston, 'will be happy to receive Young Ladies either as Boarders or as Day Pupils, and trusts by unremitting attention to their moral and intellectual improvement to merit the same patronage she had hitherto obtained in the colony'. When the notice advising the return date for the students for the second half of 1869 appeared later in the year there were 'vacancies for two or three boarders'. It is mainly through such advertisements that we are able to trace Matilda's fortunes in these years.

When she returned to North Adelaide, Matilda joined the flourishing Baptist Church, and attended regularly there for the rest of her life. She was there for the exciting time of the laying of the foundation stone of the new church in Tynte Street in December 1869, a building for which George Fife Angas had contributed £570. Later the church hall and manse were erected. These buildings are still an important part of the streetscape of Tynte Street, though the manse no longer functions as a minister's residence.

Towards the end of 1869, the year in which she returned to Adelaide, Matilda's next novel, *Silken Cords and Iron Fetters*, began to appear, and the fact that the first half of it is set in Adelaide, in North Adelaide in fact—Margaret Street—and that it shows an interest in comparing the town of 1852 with the town of the 1860s, suggests that it was not begun until Matilda had returned to city living. The earlier novels did sometimes record brief visits to Adelaide, the suburbs or 'the Bay', but they were all essentially country novels.

But even though she had returned to the city her new novel was published in a country town and by someone she had known for many years. *Silken Cords* began serialisation in *The Gawler Times and Goldfields Reporter* in November of 1869 and continued until May 1870. *The Gawler Times* was a new paper set up and edited by John Baptist Austin, son of the Reverend J. B. Austin. The younger John Austin had been for much of his life a writer and lecturer about mines and mining, and this was a new venture. Matilda's novel was announced in an editorial on 5 November, in which the first episode appeared—'We also fulfil our promise to furnish a tale by a well-known and admired author'. This gives an indication of Matilda's standing in the community, as well as of Austin's respect for her.

Silken Cords is set in the 1850s, at the time of the gold discoveries at Ballarat. Most of the action of the novel takes place in Adelaide, but as one might have expected of Matilda in a novel written for the *Goldfields Reporter*, some of it is set at the diggings. She takes the reader by boat to Melbourne and hence to the Ballarat canvas town. The narrator remarks that life at the diggings—'with all its usual accompaniments of the rude, the wild and perilous'—'is now a familiar picture to the Australian mind, if not to the dweller in the homeland'. Nevertheless she provides some details of the life.

Though she had not been to the goldfields herself she had a ready source of information in her brothers. William and Frederick had both spent some time prospecting, and Henry had spent over ten years in the Bendigo area. By 1869 he was married and living in the old prospecting town of Inglewood in Victoria, where he was a journalist, secretary of the local hospital, a share-broker and a general agent. He had strong feelings for his siblings and had made several trips back to South Australia. And Emily too had visited Inglewood.

Like most of Matilda's stories, *Silken Cords* has the flimsiest of plots. The strong godly young man who is the protagonist and whose ill health makes an outdoor life essential finds gold in small but sufficient quantities at the diggings; his weak, easily-led and discontented young friend is led astray and loses both health and fortune. When he is finally restored to his family he is a sadder and wiser young man.

Once again Matilda's object is to suggest how hard it is for the young to maintain steadfast and moral behaviour without the strength which belief in Christ will give them. She does not preach sermons however, and the mild story was received with some satisfaction by local reviewers. The editor of *Truth and Progress*, who had been sent a copy by John Austin, wrote that

> We think … the authoress has done well in choosing a new sphere and a fresh class of characters. The country with its gum trees, and farms, and townships—its chapels, and ministers, and congregations—she has fully worked; and it is quite a pleasing surprise to meet with her in the streets of Adelaide, and among the young men and the families who live in and around the city.

This Baptist clergyman thoroughly recommended the book. Others were beginning to find Matilda's stories too lacking in incident and subtlety to attract robust or literary tastes. The reviewer in *The Athenaeum* in London—the English edition appeared at the end of 1870—while admitting that the story was 'calculated to do good to young boys who think it manly to cast off restraint, and to go on in their own way', nevertheless noted that it was a 'story that Sunday-School libraries might admit to their shelves without fear of encouraging an illicit taste for fiction'.

Silken Cords was published in book form by the publishers of *The Gawler Times*, Whaley, Austin, & Co., midway through 1870. This attractive little volume bears an advertisement for 'Angaston House: Institution for Young Ladies' which adds a little to our knowledge. It gives an indication of what was taught in Matilda's school: 'The Usual Branches of English, with Music, French, German, Drawing, &c'. That 'particular attention' was to be paid to the 'Moral and Mental Training' of the young ladies was only to be expected of Matilda's school. More interesting is the note about fees. Board and Education was £40 per annum; for Day Pupils it was £6. As happens today allowance was made if there was more than one member of a family.

Apparently Matilda's school met with success, for in 1873 she moved to larger premises across the road on the north side of Buxton Street just a little west of where she had been at first. This more substantial property had a rateable value of £45. Throughout that time the advertisements noting the return date at the beginning of each quarter reveal that there were sometimes vacancies for one or two or even three young ladies as boarders. In 1878 the fees increased to 10 guineas, that is £10 10s., per quarter.

As might be expected Matilda kept on writing, although the beginning of this period of her life was not so productive. Perhaps she was not in such need and could proceed with less compulsion, or perhaps the city school took more of her time to administer.

Her next full length book did not appear until 1874, but from 1870 until 1875 she contributed occasional poems and other devotional writings to *Truth and Progress*, the South Australian Baptist journal. She also wrote a serial, *Jem's Hopes; and What They*

Grew To, for *The South Australian Temperance Herald* towards the end of 1872. It is a tale which has much in common with the 'waif' stories of Sara Smith ('Hesba Stretton'), whose most famous story *Jessica's First Prayer* had appeared in England in 1867. There can be no doubt that Matilda had read and been influenced by Sara Smith's work.

In *Jem's Hopes* Maggie and Jem are friends of the gutter, existing in poverty and misery in the slums of Adelaide. Jem is drawn one night by the lights in a chapel, and the sound of singing, to enter and listen. He hears a temperance lecture which inspires him with energy and determination, and he begins to make his way by the house-to-house selling of wooden pegs which he has carved himself. Both his family and Maggie's are ruined by drink, and Maggie appears to be consumptive through malnutrition. For us, the story ends here, because unfortunately only four episodes are extant. The files of *The South Australian Temperance Herald* are incomplete.

The final great productive period of Matilda's writing life began with the appearance of *John's Wife*, published in England in 1874. It was the first of the six novels she wrote between 1874 and 1880, and the first of three more temperance novels. The early copies of *John's Wife* bear no date of publication, but the book was being advertised in Adelaide papers in September and it was reviewed in *The South Australian Chronicle and Mail Weekly* (hereafter *The Chronicle*) on 19 September 1874.

It is the most startling of Matilda's stories. It deals with alcoholism which not only leads to death, but almost to murder. In this novel, for the first time, the narrator is not the confident Maud Jeanne Franc, but a diffident and rather ineffectual young woman named Milly Ashwin, who conducts a little school in her own home and spends most of her life worrying about her brother John and his wife Mabel. Mabel is always regarded with some suspicion by Milly, who is unwilling to yield her brother to married life. Milly makes an effort to be fair and we are told that Mabel's mother died when she was young and that her father has always indulged her. But Milly's worst fears are realised when Mabel's wilfulness and craving for excitement lead her eventually to chronic alcoholism. In a fit of delirium she tries to strangle her young son, and almost succeeds, and although under strict supervision eventually manages to destroy herself.

In spite of the unsatisfactory nature of the narrator, whom I cannot help thinking Matilda thought to be a more sympathetic character than I can find her, the story of *John's Wife* is truly horrifying. The review in *The Chronicle* has some criticisms of the style of the book, but none of its subject matter. 'We wish we could think the picture overdrawn, but too many sad instances have come under our notice from which, without exaggeration, such a tale as this might be woven, that the main incidents may well be founded on fact.' There were indeed many responsible citizens in the colony who were concerned about the problems caused by the ready availability of cheap strong colonial wine. It was in this year that the inaugural meetings for the Inebriate Asylum were held.

Matilda's next book, *Hall's Vineyard*, requested by Angaston citizens and published in 1875, was a novel which set out to show that winegrowing inevitably led to alcoholism, disaster and ultimately death. *John's Wife* had been a city novel, with John and Mabel living in a house on South Terrace—'a really nice one, standing back in a large old garden'. In *Hall's Vineyard* Matilda returned to the country for her setting, and to the time of the 1850s.

It is another pioneering story in which two brothers, Ben and Dick Hall and their families, arrive in South Australia, take up virgin land somewhere north of Mount Pleasant, and begin to farm. Ben starts a dairy, Dick a vineyard. The dairy prospers, but the vineyard leads to alcoholism in Dick and his sons, the ill treatment and death of his wife, his daughter-in-law and her baby, and finally to ruin. The novel ends with some fierce words about drinking:

> This is, alas! no overdrawn picture we have portrayed to our readers. Our daily papers teem with accounts of the evils of intemperance in all its hideous forms,—with details of the crushed limb or crushed out life; of the murderous action or suicide's rash deed; with accidents of all kinds, and disgraceful

conduct of all characters; and all attributable to the one dire curse,—intoxicating drink!

Hall's Vineyard, p. 264

Unfortunately it is still true that such things can be found in our daily papers. Matilda's solution of total abstinence has not been found to be the answer. In this novel she does present characters who are able to drink in moderation, but puts forward her belief that in so doing they 'throw a stumbling block' in the way of those weaker than themselves and become 'in some measure responsible' for their fall.

Hall's Vineyard was followed towards the end of 1877 by her last temperance novel, *Little Mercy, or For Better, For Worse*. The vineyards this time are in the foothills east of Adelaide, and are, like the vines uprooted at Evandale by Sarah Evans, pulled up when the young owner is convinced by the trials of his sister Mercy and his own excesses in drinking and gambling that the use of alcohol cannot be justified. Mercy's husband begins as a moderate drinker but is soon drinking to excess and wasting his time and resources. He loses his money and his house and finally, a victim of delirium tremens, is instrumental in causing the death of his daughter. Mercy's continued devotion to him leads him to endeavour to make a new start in England where he has family who will help him.

Matilda was not, however, exclusively occupied with the temperance issue. Before the appearance of *Little Mercy*, a new serial, *'Two Sides to Every Question' from a South Australian Standpoint*, written expressly for the *The Illustrated Adelaide News*, began to appear. It ran in Adelaide from January 1876 until February 1877 and came out in book form in London in 1883.

Two Sides has nothing of the singleness of purpose of the temperance novels. It raises a number of issues, and as the title suggests presents two sides to each. Speculation is one of them and marriage another. Even money may be a curse as well as a blessing. The novel shows too that there is something besides teaching which a educated gentlewoman might take up when in extremity. When Nettie Alton's farmer father dies, leaving nothing but debts, starting a school is not an option. 'There are so few children about here, and the Government school takes up what there is.' Owning one of the early sewing-machines, a 'Wheeler and Wilson', she sews for the shops and for private clients until her brother is able to contribute to the family income and she finds a suitable husband herself. Brother, sister and invalid mother all suffer in their pride at the necessity for Nettie to do such work but she does not believe the work dishonourable and she is not demeaned by it.

Another serial, *No Longer a Child*, was soon to appear in *The Leader*, a Melbourne paper. It ran from October 1878 until August 1879. Once again it is clear that Matilda has carefully adapted her material to her audience. This novel, appearing in an important and influential Melbourne weekly, is the least didactic and least overtly religious of all of her works. It deals with the difficult life of a romantically-minded young girl of mixed parentage. A coarse German farmer father and a more refined English mother have different expectations for their daughter. The father sees her as a possession to be sold in marriage and the mother, who has protected her from manual work and brought her up to believe herself independent and superior, is powerless to oppose him. Problems and disappointments result ultimately in Lena's marriage to someone she cannot love, and to her early death from a combination of consumption and a broken heart.

Although this story gave Matilda the opportunity to criticise the German community—she must have had considerable contact with German migrants both in the Mount Barker-Hahndorf area and in the Barossa Valley—and she is harsh in her treatment of Lena's father and her unfeeling brothers, she was far from one-sided in her portraits of German people. Some of the kindest people in the story, the most understanding of Lena's situation, are Germans, and the coarse, uncompromising and indelicately persistent suitor whom she finally marries in despair is English.

The final novel of this period, *Beatrice Melton's Discipline*, came out in London in October of 1880, so that too was probably finished by the end of 1879. After the strength of *No Longer a Child*, which seems to me one of the best, and certainly the most powerful, of Matilda's novels, *Beatrice Melton* is rather insipid. First-person narration, which is again used here, was a technique which did not suit Matilda. Maud Jeanne Franc could speak with confidence and authority; Matilda's first-person female voices are tentative, irritatingly introspective and missish. I cannot believe that Matilda was at all like that herself. Beatrice Melton writing of her inability to forgive God for taking her father's life (in exactly the same manner and circumstances as Matilda's own husband had been taken) is a diffident, self-conscious, martyrish kind of person. It is impossible to imagine Beatrice taking up her pen and writing in the decisive way Maud Jeanne Franc does.

It seems to me that Matilda did not want to use a personality like the one she had created for Franc when she used first-person narration, and that she failed to find a different convincing voice. Beatrice keeps a small school with a few boarders and day-pupils, looks after the children of a widower whom she admires, and finally, after obtusely and irritatingly failing to see his affection, marries him. In a way the novel suggests that Matilda had run out of ideas and energy. She must have written with enormous perseverance to have achieved what she did in those years. Now perhaps she was tired.

She had worked very hard throughout her life and as far as her writing was concerned particularly hard during the seventies. She had written twelve full-length novels in twenty years, and had brought up four children. She was a well-known and respected schoolmistress, proprietor of a school now known as Angaston House Establishment for Young Ladies. This name looks impressive even now, as it leads the columns of newspaper advertisements for return dates under the heading 'Education'.

One can hope that she was now no longer in financial difficulties. Many of her novels had been serialised locally and almost all had been or were to be published in England as well. In addition she had had a small windfall from her husband's estate. Something —conceivably a share certificate—which had been valueless when Ephraim died, had now proved to be of sufficient value for it to be necessary for Letters of Administration to be applied for to clear Ephraim's effects for probate. On 1 November 1879 Letters of

Administration were granted to Matilda for an estate of about £50.

In January 1880 an advertisement announced that 'Mrs E. Evans, having moved to a Large and New House, a few doors from her late residence, is prepared to receive additional pupils after the Vacation'. It must have been a much larger house for its rateable value was £70. It was in Buxton Street, on the same side as the last house which was valued at only £45, but nearer Jeffcott Street. In spite of this improvement the fees of £10 10s. per quarter did not change.

There was a great deal of work to be done in this move, not only in the house, but also in the garden. Matilda wrote to her niece Emily, aged ten, who was still living in Victoria with her family, and told her about it late in 1879. Since there are so few letters of Matilda's in existence it is worth quoting in full. It gives a fleeting glimpse of her world.

> Angaston House
> North Adelaide
> Nov 17/79
>
> My dear Emily,
> I am glad that you think Mama & Papa will spare you to me for a bit—we will take all manner of care of you and love you very much if you do come.
> We are going to live in a nice large new house, but as it is new the garden is not yet laid out—perhaps you may help to put plants in. There is plenty of room for a play ground. We shall soon get a nice garden.
> I have never been to the Waterfalls. Very likely we may all go some day together. Your cousins Harry and Willie will like to have you with them. They are quite young men but they will like to pet their cousin Emily I know—it will be like having a sister.
> I am sorry that I have no Photo to send you. I will send Mama one, tell her as soon as I can have one taken—which will be soon.
> I have a nice little girl—a boarder—who you will be able to play with—she is twelve years old but only looks ten and as she is an only girl has been petted—her name is Blanch—She seemed very pleased at the thought of your coming.
> Perhaps Uncle William may come over this Christmas— then you could come with him.

I think you will be happy over here. And you can write very often to Papa and Mama and it will be something to look forward to, to go to see them and take home specimens of what you have learnt to do. And now my darling, with plenty of love and kisses I must close for I want to post this and it is late;

> Your ever loving Auntie
> Matilda Jane Evans.

Give my love to all your brothers and kiss my little namesake for me.

Although Matilda does not say so, Henry and his wife Jane, with their four little boys, Emily and their baby daughter, Florence Matilda, were soon to move to South Australia. Sometime before the end of 1880 they settled at Gawler, where Henry was a mining manager and journalist. He became editor of *The Gawler Standard* and later of *The Bunyip*, another Gawler paper, when it merged with the *Standard*.

It seems from Matilda's letter that Emily was to attend Angaston House as a boarder, at least for a time. It must have meant a great deal to Matilda to have her brother and his family so close. Sadly, Florence, Matilda's 'little namesake', died on 18 April 1881 at the age of two after a 'sharp illness'. Two days later Matilda wrote to Emily at Gawler:

> My dear little Emmy, I have felt so much for you all - Auntie and I have been grieved enough but poor Papa and Mama - and all of you - it must have been terrible - only it is a comfort to know that our darling Flossie is safe in the Arms of Jesus - and that one day we shall see her again.

The letter makes it clear that both Matilda and her sister Emily were teachers in the Angaston House school, for Matilda told Emmy that the telegram bearing the news of Flossie's death had made both of them 'quite unfit for teaching'. They were glad that it was only the first day of the school term and that not many pupils had come.

Harry and Willie, Matilda's sons, were now growing up. At the beginning of 1880 Harry was nineteen and Willie seventeen. They had both been educated at one of Adelaide's leading schools, the North Adelaide Grammar School, later known as Whinham College, which was in Ward Street, North Adelaide. John Whinham, the headmaster, did not live at the school, but in a house in Buxton Street almost opposite Matilda.

Both boys had literary talents and aspirations, and both later became journalists on the staff of *The South Australian Advertiser*. Harry eventually became proprietor and editor of *Quiz*, an Adelaide literary journal renowned for its wit and verve, which he and a friend started in 1889. But before that, towards the end of the 1870s, just after he left Whinham College, Harry brought out a small literary journal. Both Harry and Willie and 'Cit', who in the early 1900s wrote the 'Town Tattle' column for *The Bunyip* at Gawler, contributed to Harry's first youthful magazine, the cost of which was borne by Matilda. It is pleasant to know that she had enough money both to send her boys to a leading private school, and later to encourage their literary ambitions.

She herself of course continued writing and in 1880 began her association with *The Christian Colonist*, a proselytising paper which had begun in 1878. In the next few years she wrote a number of long stories for the *Colonist*, stories which have little plot and deal specifically with characters learning to understand how to live as Christians. 'Into the Light' and its sequel 'Walking in the Light' were later published together in London under the title *Into the Light*, but the other stories, 'The Burdens of Life and How to Bear Them' and 'Wooden Crosses', have never been republished.

Another writing project of this time was a short story, 'Ellie Venn and What Christmas Brought to Her', for the *South Australian Christmas Annual*, a collection of Christmas pieces collected by the South Australian journalist and author George Loyau and published in time for Christmas 1881. Loyau's venture seems to have been insufficiently successful for him to be keen to try again, but for Christmas 1882 Matilda and her son William made a similar attempt.

Christmas Bells, edited by Maude Jeanne Franc, contains two longish poems by W. J. Evans and three stories, two of them, 'Unexpected: A Christmas Week's Experience' and 'In His Right Mind: A Tale of Christmas Eve', by Maude Jeanne Franc, and one unsigned. The unsigned story 'Captain Peter Brown's Christmas' is almost certainly by Harry. He was a great humorist as his published writings show and the jocular style of this story is very like his. It appears that this little book was a family undertaking with Matilda encouraged by and encouraging her sons, both of whom wished to become writers. They did not attempt such a thing again; probably the returns were not worth the effort.

More successful were the stories written for the Christmas Supplements of *The Chronicle*. 'Tom Morison's Golden Christmas', a tale of the rescue of fallen fortunes by the finding of gold on a property in the country not far from Adelaide, was the first of six long tales—two in 1884—which appeared in successive Christmas Supplements. The last was already in the hands of the publisher when Matilda died in October 1886. These stories show Matilda writing for a different audience. Although clearly based on the Christian faith they are secular stories, without sermons. They are set, except for isolated incidents, in the country, where obviously Matilda's heart always was, and deal with the problems of pioneering South Australian families. That she was asked to produce these stories year after year tells us something of her continued standing as an author and entertainer in Adelaide.

But although she continued to succeed as an author it is likely that she was not in good health. The one photograph I have seen of her, perhaps that taken to satisfy the request made to her by her niece Emily, shows her looking rather frail and drawn. It must have been taken round about this time when she was in her early or mid fifties. After her death many of those who wrote about her mentioned that she had not been well for some time.

Whatever the reason she suddenly gave up her school and moved round the corner into a smaller house in Wellington Square, on the southern corner of Buxton Street. The move does seem to have been sudden, for the advertisements for Angaston House Establishment appeared at usual in January 1883, but they did not reappear, as they had done for fifteen years, at the beginning of the next quarter, nor ever again. Nor did anyone else take over her school as far as I can discover. Ill health seems the most obvious reason for the change.

But other, perhaps contributing, factors suggest themselves. There were more schools being set up all the time. In 1879 the Board of Education opened an excellent girls' secondary school—the Advanced School for Girls—in Grote Street in the city. Public transport was improving, and students could travel more easily. There was more competition in North Adelaide too. The three Misses McMinn who had kept a ladies' school in Molesworth Street moved at the beginning of 1883 into the house vacated by John Whinham when the new large Whinham College opened on the corner of Ward Street and Jeffcott Street, and set up Tormore House there. This was almost opposite Angaston House. (Many years later, under Caroline Jacob, Tormore House became the leading private girls' school in Adelaide.) Matilda could well have found that competition was becoming fiercer.

More importantly Harry and Willie, at the beginning of 1883, were twenty-three and twenty-one years of age. They were now earning and could contribute to the family income instead of being a charge upon it. Perhaps they realised that their mother's constant devotion to her two professions of teaching and writing was undermining her health, and felt that they were now in a position to help her, and even, if it proved necessary, to take responsibility for her support. She was after all now fifty-five years of age, and she had lived a life of unremitting industry. Whatever the reason, the school was given up, the smaller house taken and Matilda began to give a new direction to her life.

CHAPTER 9

A Quiet Life

H enry Congreve later wrote that at this time in her life
Matilda 'entered upon a quiet life'. After the energy required
to conduct and teach in a school, a life of retirement must indeed
have seemed quiet. But Matilda had plenty to do. In the first place
she went on writing. She wrote stories for *The Christian Colonist*,
for *The Chronicle*, and a short piece for *Truth and Progress*. Novels
written earlier appeared in London and then arrived in Adelaide.
'*Two Sides to Every Question*' and *Golden Gifts* both came out in
1883 and *Into the Light*, the second part of which had appeared in
the Colonist in 1884, in 1885.

She wrote a new long novel, *The Master of Ralston*, which
showed her at the height of her powers, and that also appeared in
1885. It is not her best novel, though it is a good one, but it is a
leisurely, confident, expansive novel. Its tone is relaxed and con-
templative, suggesting that for once she had had time to stop and
think. It is set in her favourite area, the countryside and township
of Mount Barker, this time called Amber Vale. There is a little
more intricacy in the plot of this novel, which has a subplot with a
hint of mystery. Although the chief characters are once again a
farmer and a schoolteacher, there is a difference, as the farmer is a
forty-year-old wealthy bachelor who has some mental and emotional struggles as he tries to believe himself attractive to the gentle and overworked young teacher. Matilda's characters are rarely
introspective, but there is a hint in this novel that she was becoming more confident in this area.

The central incidents in the novel stem from a community
movement to raise money for the local Institute and its library.

This is in itself an interesting subject to present-day readers, giving as it does a picture of a nineteenth-century country town working for a cause. *The Master of Ralston* was the most successful of her later novels. The reviewer for *The Chronicle* thought it 'among the best, if indeed it be not the best', of her novels, and praised it for its truthful depiction of country life in South Australia, and the reviewer for the *The Observer* hoped 'to have the pleasure of welcoming further productions from the talented author'.

It seems likely that her sister Emily shared her retirement. I have not found much evidence of what Emily did after she left the school at Athelstone, but Gray and others have assumed that she spent her time with Matilda, and she is said to have been a music teacher. Music was always a part of Matilda's life and was taught in all her schools for young ladies. Her stepdaughter Pollie became a music teacher, and her niece Emily frequently performed at charity concerts when she lived at Gawler. When he wrote his Christmas recollections Henry Congreve remembered the sound of the piano in his sister's house. Emily may well have been the music teacher in Matilda's schools or she may indeed have taught other subjects.

The letter written by Matilda to her niece Emmy after the death of little Florence in 1881 refers to Emily as teaching in the school and a later letter in 1885 makes it clear that Emily was living with Matilda and the boys, although she was at that particular moment travelling in Victoria. In both letters mention is made of her poor health.

Emily's Will shows her to have left a much larger estate than Matilda, which suggests that she had had a steady source of income over the years. She did not of course have children to support as Matilda did. She did not make a lasting impression with her writings, but she published with the same publishers and papers as Matilda, which also suggests that they worked and lived together. *Colonial Pen-Scratchings*, Emily's collection of acerbic short stories about colonial life, was published in 1860, the year after *Marian*, and by the same publisher, Alfred Waddy, at Mount Barker. Her novel *Floy*, like Matilda's *Golden Gifts*, came out in

The Kapunda Herald. During the early 1880s, when Matilda was writing stories for *The Christian Colonist*, Emily was contributing poems to the same publication. In 1884 some of her poems appeared in *Truth and Progress*, a journal to which Matilda had contributed since 1870. Emily also published poems in *The South Australian Advertiser*.

Matilda's other great interest in this period of her quiet life was her church work. She had been a member of the North Adelaide Baptist Church in Tynte Street for many years. In the October of 1883, the year in which she gave up the school, she was elected a deaconess of the Church and became secretary for the deaconesses' meetings. I have no doubt that Matilda enjoyed contributing to the work of the Church, though deaconesses had little real power and the meetings were always chaired by the pastor. In general the duties of the deaconesses were to supervise the cleaning and furnishings of the Church and its adjacent offices, to make arrangements for such functions as the Anniversary Tea Meetings and to visit the sick.

When the number of deaconesses was increased to eight, each was allotted a special district for visiting. Mrs Evans took Bowden-on-the-Hill, Ovingham and the west side of Prospect. If no transport was provided this would have entailed a great deal of walking. Still, a horse-drawn cab might have been hired for 5s. or so an hour. In the last year of her life, 1886, Matilda left Wellington Square and moved with the boys, and probably Emily, to Clifton Street in Prospect. This would at least have moved her much nearer to the area to be visited.

The minutes of the meetings of deaconesses not only provide information about her services to the Church but also record that after her death—and she was still the secretary at the time of her death—a window in her memory was placed in the Church, on the west side. Unfortunately there is now no such memorial, and nothing is known of what must once have been there.

Earlier than this, on 8 January 1885, she wrote a newsy letter to her niece Emmy in Gawler which throws much light on her activities and her state of mind at the time. The Gawler family had obviously all been with her and her own family at Christmas, although 'Auntie Emily' was travelling in Victoria and thinking of going on to Sydney—'I think it is not at all wise her doing so in her health'. Her brother James was with her and his health, like Emily's, was poor. She had received a letter from England from her niece Minnie, her half-brother George's youngest daughter, who had just been married and sent photos. She had seen her step-daughter Pollie and Pollie's first child little Lilly who 'can run alone and chatter away finely'. Pollie was coming to Adelaide for a week and wanted Matilda to go back to Tarcowie with her— 'perhaps I may'.

More importantly 'I very much wish to begin teaching again'. She wanted Emmy to ask her father for his opinion because her own sons 'vehemently' opposed the idea. This supports my belief that it was an illness or at least ill health which forced her to give up the school two years earlier. In this letter she shows herself full of vigour and desire to teach and rather humiliated at feeling herself subject to her sons' prohibition. In the last few weeks she had received three unsolicited enquiries about her terms from people desirous of sending their children to her school—'after two years rest!' This says much for her standing in the community as a teacher. She told Emmy that she felt obliged reluctantly to give up the idea for a time, at least 'while we are in this house'. But the wish was there and it seems to me the necessary energy as well. Maybe it was further ill health which prevented her from once more opening a school.

The years when Matilda was associated with the North Adelaide Baptist Church were active ones, and she obviously contributed a great deal to the life of the Church. She had been ill with what is described in obituaries as a painful internal disease for some time before her death, but even when unwell persisted in serving the Church to the limit of her strength.

She died on Friday, 22 October 1886, of peritonitis, and was buried on the following Sunday in the West Terrace Cemetery by the minister of the North Adelaide Baptist Church, the Reverend W.E. Rice. On Sunday morning, 31 October, Mr Rice preached a special sermon in her honour. After speaking of her work as Maud Jeanne Franc, he spoke of his personal respect for her:

In her death we have lost a valued friend and a devoted helper in the work of the Lord. Those of us who knew her best loved her most. Her quiet, unassuming, gentle disposition captivated our affection, and I believe I give expression to the feelings of the members of this Church generally when I say we didn't know how much we loved her until she was taken away from us. We mourn our loss and deeply do we sympathize with her bereaved children and the other members of her family. But while her death to us is 'loss', to her it is 'gain'. When for a few minutes I was permitted to see her in her extreme weakness, and with that thoughtfulness which characterized her whole life she told me I had helped her to attain the rest of faith, I felt and do feel that if I had lived and preached only to help upwards and heavenwards such a one as 'Maud Jeanne Franc' it were worth living for.

Coming from someone who obviously knew her well but was not a member of her family these words seem to me to carry a great deal of weight. Yet all of the obituaries, in the country as well as in the Adelaide papers, speak of her in the same way. There is respect and admiration for her industry and achievement as Maud Jeanne Franc—'a pleasant writer of homely stories'— and praise for the gentleness and piety of the woman. Her gentle disposition and quiet retiring nature are the two qualities constantly stressed. They are qualities which are not those usually met with in headmistresses, and I believe tell us something of the quality of her schools. Her gentle authority, combined with her great faith, her determination and her ability to persevere, as well as with her quiet sense of fun and her belief in laughter, must have made her schools good places to be. She was a loving and lovable woman. But it is pleasing to see that *The Register* noted that although quiet, she could be vivacious in conversation! According to their friends her sons were great wits, and their writings support this. I think Matilda's must have been a bright and fun-loving home.

The greatest tribute came from her brother Henry in the obituary he wrote at Gawler for *The Bunyip*:

Naturally of a retiring disposition, only a select circle of friends were enabled to appreciate the full value of her character. Utterly unselfish, she lived only for others, and even within a few minutes of her death was her marvellous love for others and her self-forgetfulness displayed. As a daughter, sister, wife, mother, or friend she was everything that could be wished. Having lived a good Christian life, her end was in keeping. Looking death full in the face, not a cloud or doubt darkened her mind, but she dropped asleep, relying on the promises and love of God.

When Henry's obituary was reprinted in *The Chronicle* this paragraph was omitted; it evidently seemed to the editor to be altogether too fulsome. But to me it seems a genuine attempt to convey deep and strong feelings. It is not in this way that we generally hear brothers speak of sisters. Henry's words carry conviction to me, and have coloured my view of Matilda's life and work.

Another testimony to the strength and sweetness of Matilda's disposition can be found in the characters of her sons. Both boys died young and unmarried, Harry in January, 1899 at the age of thirty-eight, and Willie in September, 1904, at the age of forty-two. They were both talented journalists, entertaining literary men, with wide circles of friends. Harry died suddenly of pneumonia which developed from a cold caught when the weather changed while he was on a bicycle ride in the hills. Willie had suffered from gout for years and had experienced pain consistently, but his death was like his father's from a paralytic stroke.

What is most striking about the comments made on the deaths of these two young men is the affection in which they were held. They were vivacious and witty, it is true, but consistently kind. Harry 'overflowed with the milk of human kindness', and the list of prominent people who attended his funeral is quite staggering. It included the Premier, the Speaker of the House of Assembly, the Commissioner of Crown Lands, the Mayor of Adelaide, and the Under Treasurer, besides a great many relatives and friends. There were also many apologies.

That her sons were so much admired and loved when they had had only their own personalities and talents to help them make their mark in South Australia, underlines Matilda's strengths as a woman and mother. She was not just a fine woman. They were a fine family.

Matilda had made a will in the June of 1886 in which she bequeathed the copyrights of her last two books, *Into the Light* and *The Master of Ralston* to her sons. She said she held the agreement for those two. Of the others she speaks of her 'share' in the copyright, and it is not clear what she meant by this. But perhaps she still received some income from Sampson Low, her publishers. If she had no such expectations her financial position was not good, for when she died her whole estate amounted to under £100.

She asked her sons as executors to give some article by which they might remember her to her brothers and stepchildren. To Emily she left £25—a quarter of her estate—her clothes, her Canary, and 'all Miss Warner's books'. (Susan Warner, whose pseudonym was Elizabeth Wetherell, was an American writer of domestic religious tales. Her most famous book, *The Wide Wide World*, had been published in 1851. Her books had obviously been models for Matilda.)

Emily outlived Matilda by ten years, living in, and expecting to die in, lodgings, as her Will indicates. She did however go to stay with her brother Henry for her last days. By 1893 Henry had retired from the editorship of *The Bunyip* and had come to Adelaide to live in Palm Place, near St Peter's College. He had been a Presbyterian lay preacher for many years and was soon to become an Elder of Chalmers (now Scots) Church, in North Terrace, Adelaide.

Emily died at Henry's home on 28 September 1896 of cancer. Her will disclosed that she left £975, a considerable sum in those days. She left small legacies to Henry and William, to her niece Emily, to her sister-in-law, to the inmates of the Destitute Asylum, to the Bible Society and to the Norwood and Adelaide poor. The residue of her estate was to be divided between her brothers, Henry, William, Frederick and James.

Her first request in her Will, however, was to be buried with her father and sister in the West Terrace Cemetery. She directed that an iron railing should be placed around the plot and a headstone erected, inscribed with the names of her father, her mother, her sister and herself. She asked for 'the names and dates of death only with the added words "In hope of Eternal life"'.

Her wishes were only partly carried out. The headstone which can be seen in the Cemetery now bears the words

In loving memory of
Henry Congreve
Died 1852   Aged 59 years
Elizabeth Ann Congreve
(wife) Died at sea, 1852 Aged 49 years
Mrs E Evans (Maud Jeanne Franc)
Died 1886   Aged 59 years
Emily Congreve
Died 1896   Aged 66 years
Both Daughters of the Above
All died in the hope of the glorious resurrection

In June 1899 a second headstone was added to this plot:

Sacred to the memory
of
Henry Congreve Evans
(Quiz)
Died 9 January 1899
Aged 38 years
Erected by his friends and admirers

And later still a third:

Erected by old Comrades
in Memory of William James Evans
Died 22nd September 1904
Aged 42 years.

Even these headstones speak of the affection in which these boys were held, for the stones were not erected by relatives and descendants but by friends, admirers and comrades.

Henry Congreve, Matilda's brother, lived until 1918, the last twenty years of his life at his house 'Stretton' on Walkerville Road (now Stephen Terrace) St Peters. Frederick and William both died at 'Stretton'. Frederick, who had been living at Meningie, died in September 1906. William, who had returned from Victoria in 1894 and had lived in retirement at Bridgewater, sometimes in the company of his younger brother James, died in July 1907. All three were buried in the Payneham Cemetery. James moved to Sydney in the early 1900s, but he died in Brisbane, aged 94, in July 1934.

As a family the Congreves had contributed much to the life of South Australia. Henry believed that Matilda's work would live on: ' "Maud Jeanne Franc" has gone, but has left her work behind to tell on future generations'. Matilda's novels have not proved to have qualities which would make them acceptable to readers today, but they were popular for many years and were frequently reprinted. And they can today tell us much of past times. The next section tells of the world which is revealed in Matilda's novels.

PART TWO

The Novelist and Her World

Decorative silver stamping for the 1888–1895 uniform edition.

CHAPTER 10

Sweet Stories

The novels of Maud Jeanne Franc are not remembered today, nor are they readily available to readers and students who might enjoy them or gain some knowledge from reading them. I propose to consider first why they have lost favour and how far they are still worth reading, and then to give some idea of the world they reflect and of the relationship to it of Matilda Evans, schoolteacher and writer. I will also attempt to discover who read these novels and why.

Franc's novels were popular: they were advertised, they sold, they were reprinted. They were extensively reviewed, at first with excitement and respect. But as time went on, although the sales remained high the enthusiasm of reviewers became markedly less. This is 'another of Maud Jean Franc's sweet stories' wrote a reviewer in a short notice of *Into The Light* in *The Observer* in May 1885. The lack of any detailed reference to character or incident in this little review suggests that the reviewer had not read the book, though he had looked at it—he knew at least that it was in two parts. He probably had not read any other of Matilda's novels either, for 'sweet stories' is a loose and derogatory generalisation which damns with faint praise. The patronising male tone, the lack of knowledge, the easy dismissal—'The story is essentially religious and will appeal especially to the sympathies of that class.' —help us to understand how it came about that Matilda's work is so little known today. She had been much read and was still being read well into the 1920s but by the middle of the twentieth century what she had written was either devalued or forgotten.

Ignorance, concentration on what interests male readers, and perhaps a conviction that what is 'popular' is bound to be negligible, especially if the writer is female, have helped contribute to the disappearance of Maud Jeanne Franc from the list of Australian writers. E. Morris Miller's great bibliography, *Australian Literature from its Beginnings to 1935*, first published in 1940, listed her works (albeit with some errors) and treated them seriously, making a point which has seldom been made since: 'these novels represent features of the religious life of small Australian communities which do not ordinarily appear in unalloyed sincerity in what may be termed the novels of literature.' Miller, however, stressed the connection with Sunday School libraries and young people and implied that Franc's novels were scarcely worth adult attention.

H.M. Green in *A History of Australian Literature* (1961), which has been for many years the standard work on the subject, not only ignored Franc's contribution to Australian writing but referred to her contemptuously in a way that exposed his lack of knowledge of her work. Writing of what he saw as the general inferiority of Australian magazines in the mid-nineteenth century he remarked that

> Unfortunately, most of the editors failed to realize their opportunities; they could not always handle even their own Australian material: for instance a reviewer in the *Victorian Monthly Magazine* of 1859 was capable of suggesting that a book by Maud Jean Franc, a cheaply sentimental popular novelist of the day, might be the work of Catherine Helen Spence.
> (p. 295)

The review in question—as Green would have known if he had read it with attention—was of the first part only of Franc's first novel *Marian* which by July 1959, a month after its appearance, had reached Melbourne in what was—astonishingly—a second edition. The reviewer expressed amazement at the quality of *Marian* as so many other reviewers had done, seeing it essentially as a praiseworthy colonial venture.

> An Australian novel, the scene, the characters, and the incidents, all thoroughly colonial, is so unexpected a production

that we hardly know how to welcome it. We have been so accustomed to look for all our literature to European sources that a native of the soil is glanced at with more suspicion than pleasure, and we prove to our adventurous authors, with greater force than generosity—often than justice—that a man may be a prophet anywhere more easily than in his own country and among his own kindred. It was with some such laggard welcome that we took up the neatly printed cover in which the first part of the tale of Marian is enclosed, and we confess with shame, that we at first felt more surprise than pleasure at the grace and spirit that speedily became apparent in the narrative. As we proceeded in our perusal the sense of gratification gradually subdued all other feelings, and when we reached the end we were sorry that it came so soon. There is something so genial, so natural, so fresh, in the book, that its publication in any of the colonies is a thing to be proud of, and we most heartily congratulate our South Australian friends that they have shown their appreciation by calling for a second edition.

The South Australian setting and the naturalness and freshness of the writing were what prompted the reviewer to ask in a footnote 'Does the authoress of Clara Morrison know anything of Marian?' It was not an inappropriate question as the strong evangelical theme which might have alerted the reviewer to the fact that the author was not Catherine Spence did not appear in Part 1. In fact the first part of *Marian*, with its celebration of the excitement of entering on a new life in a new colony, is not sentimental; it is in fact one of the most delightful pieces Matilda ever wrote, and neither it nor the reviewer deserved Green's sneer.

Another landmark, Grahame Johnston's *Annals of Australian Literature*, which appeared first in 1970 inexplicably omitted Franc's name altogether. Her name was included in Joy Hooton and Harry Heseltine's 1992 second edition of *Annals*, but even then *Marian* was misdated by two years and of the three other works mentioned only *Emily's Choice* was one of her major works. *John's Wife* was not one of those most frequently reprinted and the little anthology of stories and poems *Christmas Bells* is the slightest of all her books. It was never reprinted but perhaps found favour in the editors' eyes because of the contribution made by her son William James Evans.

Judith Nancarrow's 1963 thesis *A Social History of South Australia 1865-1875*, which is much read by today's students, states that 'Catherine Helen Spence was "the" South Australian writer of the period, her best-known novel being *Clara Morison*'. In fact at this period the novels of Maud Jeanne Franc were appearing frequently, they were much advertised and reviewed, and were stocked by all the bookshops. Spence's novels on the other hand were in short supply and were too expensive for the general reader. Looking back we might see Spence, altogether a more 'literary' writer than Franc, as *the* writer of the period, but at the time Franc was making far more impact.

Paul Depasquale in his pioneer work *A Critical History of South Australian Literature 1836-1930* published in 1978 broke new ground by writing at some length of Franc's novels, but perhaps because of his male viewpoint and his distaste for her religious and temperance preoccupations he could see little that was positive in her work. He criticised her for 'hold[ing] up England as an ideal Christian society' and for constantly slanting her writing towards an English readership, neither of which she does. In fact some of her novels are so much aimed at local readers—*Hall's Vineyard* for instance with its attacks on winegrowers and the making and drinking of 'strong colonial wine'—that it is surprising that they were published in England at all. It is true that the characters she writes of who are newly arrived in the colony look at things initially through English eyes. What else could they do? But they are soon thoroughly immersed in the new world and do not look back to the past, unless indeed they are unsatisfactory people and return to England after having failed in their lives here. Her characters are never here to make fortunes and then return to England as so many settlers did in reality. In *No Longer A Child*, originally written for and published in *The Leader*, a Melbourne paper, she deliberately celebrated South Australia, and attacked those who made comparisons with the older country.

> The fact is, we South Australians are not half proud enough of our country, with its rapidly growing buildings, its wealth of minerals, developed or undeveloped, its thousand-and-one improvements, and its immense capabilities. We do not make

> as much capital of its wealth as we should. We allow ourselves
> to be too easily crushed by the idle comparisons of the 'newly
> arrived'; idle comparisons, for what sense is there in comparing
> the position or possessions of a country of many centuries'
> duration with one whose very existence was not dreamt of a
> hundred years ago.
>
> *No Longer A Child*, p. 71

Depasquale also criticised Franc for her 'grotesquely simplistic
psychology', 'naked religious prejudices' and the 'Calvinism which
extends its dead hand over [her] novels'. These are serious charges
and there is truth in them. But it is not the whole story. There is
plenty of joy and excitement and love of life in Franc's novels,
and there are many women characters who, for all their seeming
dependence and superficial fragility, are tough and determined.
The psychology is not always as simplistic as at first appears.

The religious beliefs, however extreme they may seem to some
readers today, were deeply and earnestly held. They were central
to the existence of the author. And since so many of the colonists
of both sexes shared her religious views this only serves to make
the novels more interesting to present-day students of early colonial days. And indeed if her work has value, it is partly here—in the
way she reflected and contributed to the religious climate of her
own day—that that value lies.

Notions of literary value have in this century tended to focus
on those aspects of texts which are timeless and universal.
Matilda's works fail in this respect. But there is another way in
which literary texts can be valued, a way which has been clearly
demonstrated by Jane Tompkins in *Sensational Designs* (1985), a
study of nineteenth-century American sentimental novels. In her
view

> … novels and stories should be studied not because they man-
> age to escape the limitations of their particular time and place,
> but because they offer powerful examples of the way a culture
> thinks about itself, articulating and proposing solutions for the
> problems that shape a particular historical moment … [they
> wish] to win the belief and influence the behaviour of the
> widest possible audience. These novelists have designs upon
> their audience, in the sense of wanting to make people think
> and act in a particular way.   p. xi

Viewed in this way Matilda's novels can be seen as addressing particular problems in colonial society—especially ways of adapting to an emerging and changing society and the questions of Godlessness and intemperance—and as addressing them with considerable success. Those who did not share Matilda's basic beliefs—that the only true reality was spiritual, that Jesus was not only Saviour but also loving friend, and that only those who had come to love and obey Him would meet again after death in a better and more beautiful world—reacted to her work in her own day much as Depasquale has more recently. For those who then shared or were sympathetic to her beliefs her novels could be valuable and influential; for those who can appreciate now how earnestly and determinedly she worked within her assumptions her novels have present as well as historical value.

Margaret Allen in her work on South Australian women writers has led the way in a reassessment of Matilda's work. In 'Domestic ideology and Maude Jeanne Franc' (*All Her Labours*, 1984) she noted similarities in the works of Matilda Evans and British and American woman writers of domestic fiction and showed how Matilda seemed 'to be responding to the dislocation caused by migration from loved English homes, and to the task of forming a respectable and stable middle class in the fluid South Australian society'. Allen saw Matilda as pointing out how necessary it was for men and women to work together at the idea of the Christian family in order to make it a reality. Matilda's concern with the abuse of alcohol was part of her attempt to strengthen family values.

> Franc was not a figure whom we would recognise as a feminist. But a corollary of total abstinence and Christianity was greater security and power within marriage for women. A shared faith in Christ meant that the husband's behaviour would be more predictable and more susceptible to the influence of the wife. A husband who abstained from drinking alcohol meant that the woman would be free from drunken rages and the poverty caused by the drinking away of wages and profits.
>
> p. 29

In the last few years Matilda's work has gained some recognition, but often the comments which are made suggest that ignorance is still a major barrier to an assessment of her contribution to Australian writing. The *Oxford Companion to Australian Literature* (1985) after stating that *Marian* 'deals with bush life' adds 'as do many others, e.g. *Emily's Choice* (1867) and *John's Wife* (1874)'. As it happens *John's Wife* is one of the few novels set almost entirely in the city, the most striking parts of the action taking place in a house on South Terrace.

By 1988, as shown in Patricia Clarke's *Pen Portraits: Women Writers and Journalists in Nineteenth-century Australia*, Matilda's achievements had begun to be accepted at least by those researching women's writing. But although Clarke acknowledged her success and her popularity she, like Morris Miller, dismissed the novels as 'moral, Sunday-school stories'. It is true that Matilda's novels were read in Sunday schools, but they reached a much wider public. At a time when strong religious views were held by a broad cross-section of the community such novels were approved family reading. And although they were usually read in editions published in England their exclusively Australian—and almost always South Australian—settings gave them a distinctive local moral focus and force.

Nobody would have read Matilda's work for the excitement of her plots or the extraordinariness of her characters. The thread of happenings is always thin and the mysteries and exciting love affairs which were the stock-in-trade of those who wrote the sentimental romances with which her novels are often classed are almost non-existent. She was interested in the world around her and how people behaved in that world, and in fact she made her stories from the fabric of the every-day life of her time. Many of her readers must have recognised this world as being very like their own. She left out a good deal and hammered away at the same few themes, but the world that she portrayed was a solid world of hard work and Christian endeavour. We know what her characters did during their working lives, how they spent their leisure time and how they thought about the things that mattered to them. Her young lovers are not shown pining with love for each other but struggling with their consciences as they try to find the moral and religious convictions which will make them worthy partners. It was this earnest approach on the part of the author which gave these novels—in the context of their times—their power.

What is least acceptable to readers today is the frequency and persistence with which the author interrupts the narrative to sermonise. Her lessons are direct, bombastic and humourless and are usually tacked on, not skilfully integrated into the story.

> Are any of our dear young readers like Katie—feeling after Christ in the darkness, seeking Him through the night, and dreading never to find Him? Take courage, dear ones, 'those that seek shall find'; that precious promise will never grow old, will never fail. The clouds shall by and by part, and the pure sunlight be revealed. You seek Jesus, and assuredly by and by you shall find Him! And ah! then for you awaits a glorious future, when you 'shall see Him as He is', with no veil between, when faith shall be exchanged for sight, and the cloud be rolled away for ever.
>
> *Vermont Vale*, p. 330

It is hard now to be sympathetic to such barefaced preaching in novels, and all of Matilda's stories have a certain amount of it. But it should be noted that the two novels which suffer most from this distracting sermonising are *Vermont Vale*, which must have been written shortly after Matilda married and when she was most under the influence of her preacher husband, and *Emily's Choice*, written not long after his death when she was in a sense celebrating their marriage and perhaps exorcising some of the traumas that the hardships of their shared lives and Ephraim's death had caused.

Another stylistic habit which detracts from the pleasure of readers today is her use of italics, not only to emphasise words which would carry an emphasis if read aloud but also to highlight key words and ideas.

> Maggie was a Scotch girl, a warm-hearted one; but she was almost more *Australian* than *Scotch*, for she remembered little of the *home* country from *personal* experience. Everything *Australian* had a double value in her eyes.
>
> *Emily's Choice*, p. 60

This irritating trait is at its worst in *Emily's Choice* which is the most sentimental and most emotionally charged of all her stories. Reviewers were displeased and perhaps their criticisms had some effect, for there are fewer examples in later novels. Interestingly the reviewer of *The Kapunda Herald* blamed the printer.

> The work is very nicely printed and choicely bound, but there is evidence of the manuscript having been that of a lady, by the presence of so many words in italic in each page, which mars the appearance of the typography. Ladies, as a rule, always underscore every word which they deem emphatic; and such marks to the printer indicate that the words so underlined are to appear in italic, although in underscoring the words in question there might have been no such intention on the part of the lady writer.

Matilda's books appealed to women and to girls, for they dealt with women's concerns and with what qualities are necessary in wives and husbands to make marriages successful. The marriage vows—'those few momentous words, so quickly spoken'—bound the partners together 'for a lifetime's happiness or a lifetime's bondage' (*Hall's Vineyard*, p. 148). This was a serious matter to Matilda, as it was to her young female readers, most of whom who had nothing to look forward to but marriage, and she did not attempt to gloss over the horrors of unions that proved unsatisfactory.

Although she does not sensationalise such incidents she makes it clear that drunken husbands physically and emotionally abuse their wives and children, and that drunken wives emotionally abuse their husbands and physically and emotionally their children. She accepted the contemporary mores of husband as bread-winner (though she herself had a life which did not fit the stereotype) and as head of the household.

But attentive reading shows that she expected women to think for themselves. Lena Hartmann fights her German father's desire that she marry a wealthy but uncouth Englishman, and tells her mother that he is 'very hard and cruel'. Mrs Hartmann answers for the father but noticeably not for herself. 'He is your father, my child, and he thinks it is right that you should do as he bids you.'

Lena's answer stresses the seriousness with which the author regarded marriage: 'And I always have till now. But this is a great thing—a thing to make one happy or wretched for life.' (*No Longer A Child*, p. 192).

It has been made clear in the story that Lena's upbringing has been at fault. She has been educated by her English mother as a 'lady' when realistically all she can look forward to is marriage to a hardworking German farmer, and has learned from unsuitable reading to indulge in romantic dreams. Nevertheless the narrator's sympathies appear to go with her as she makes her ultimately unsuccessful attempt to escape this marriage.

In *Emily's Choice* the narrator agrees with the apparently fragile clinging Emily Owen when she stands up to her pastor husband who has read her diary without permission: 'a downright theft we [the narrator] call it, and not to be tolerated even in our Glen Ness minister'. Emily appeared mollified by her husband's rather patronising apology 'but she seized the first opportunity she had to escape and to hide the little book in greater security—even beyond the reach of her husband's prying fingers' (*Emily's Choice*, pp. 103–4).

Sex, certainly a topic to interest Matilda's young readers, especially young female readers contemplating marriage, is never discussed except obliquely—although there are plenty of children! It was a taboo subject in fiction at the time and I am sure that Matilda would have believed it wrong to dwell on the kind of sexual encounters that produced 'fallen' women and illegitimate children; the newspapers of the day would have supplied her with plenty of material even if she had had no personal knowledge of such problems. It is true that there are a few obviously predatory young men in her stories but the young women who interest them are too well protected by their families and their own strong principles for them to be in any danger.

There are however instances in many of her novels of couples whose marriages are based on sexual attraction alone. Such marriages are usually disastrous. Where the parties have no religious and moral convictions in common troubles are inevitable. Some young women are strong enough to reject the young men to whom they are sexually attracted. Bessie Hall in *Hall's Vineyard* rejected her cousin Dave, though she loved him dearly, when he refused to control his drinking. He married a pliant young neighbour on the rebound and caused her death and the death of their baby. Elsie Clinton (*'Two Sides to Every Question'*) rejected the love of Arthur Delta because he was poor:

> Elsie was not fitted for a poor man's wife, and she knew it. Tenderly nurtured as she had been, surrounded by wealth, cradled in luxury, what sort of home could she have made for Arthur Delta? She liked him very much, was always happy in his company, and had he possessed riches would have gladly become his wife.
>
> *Two Sides*, p. 172

Elsie married a rich man and the narrator of the story clearly believed that—given her limitations—she did the right thing. Arthur on the other hand, unable to accept the obvious, was soon near ruin, having forged a cheque in his struggle to make himself a suitable suitor. At the news of Elsie's marriage he collapsed.

> Even in his delirium, which was not violent, but low, muttering, and distressful in its character, the name of Elsie was wailed out, mingled with agonized regret for the deed he had done, and all for *her* sake. Mines, and shares, and cheques, and Elsie, and forgery—these were the changes that were rung incessantly day and night in the ears of his anxious watchers.
>
> p. 206

Arthur is one of those who returns to England after failing to make a success of life in South Australia.

Matilda's novels depicted marriage choices realistically. She portrayed a world in which God, not man, set the standards, and lives in which hardships were inescapable. They gave women plenty to think about.

Her novels appealed to men too; men who approved of her firm religious principles and of her earnest attempts to lead unbelievers to the faith, and to men—and there were very many of them in South Australia—who shared her beliefs that only total abstinence in the whole of society would save from a horrible death those who were unable to control their drinking. But those with different views about religion and alcohol and those with different expectations as readers, who looked for intellectual and emotional power, for imagination, insight and style, or indeed for complicated plots and sensational events—all these found Matilda's tales thin and trite.

The tone of South Australian reviews of her books, which would all of course have been written by men, changed over the years from the excitement created by *Marian*, which was something new to be proud of in the colony, to the sober acceptance of her later stories as likely to please not so much the reviewer as 'admirers of the works previously written by the same authoress'.

It is worth remembering that *Marian* was an early novel of the Victorian period. It was published in the same year as George Eliot's *Adam Bede*, Dickens's *A Tale of Two Cities* and Darwin's *The Origin of Species*. As times changed values changed with them; the previously strong evangelical movement lost its force. Dissenting religious groups in South Australia lost many of their wealthy leaders, some to the United Kingdom, some to death and some to other denominations. Gradually Anglicanism became the fashionable faith and extreme views on religion and alcohol such as Matilda held seemed no longer to suit the times. The novels of Maud Jeanne Franc became less regarded, until finally the depression and the war that followed wrought such changes in society that they no longer seemed relevant.

Serious novels—and I believe Matilda was always a serious writer—are read and enjoyed because in some manner they throw light on the times and the lives of their readers. Novels that 'live' from one generation to the next, or perhaps move in and out of fashion, owe their success to the fact that they continue to interpret the times, moving somehow with the times. Whether this is the result of the skill of the writer in style plot and characterisation or the skill of the reader in probing psychological depths that may perhaps have been revealed inadvertently by the writer is really immaterial. What matters is that readers continue to learn about themselves and their own times from reading them, whatever had been the authors' intentions. Maud Jeanne Franc's novels no longer speak to our times in this way, though they remain a quarry for those who wish to go back to our past and to discover what it was like.

The Bibliography of Franc's work which appears at the end of this book and Chapter 14, 'Gentle Readers', demonstrate the impact which her work made in the past and provide the basis for my belief that study of her work will yield much useful information to students, scholars and social historians, especially those interested in the history of women.

CHAPTER 11

Work and Play – Life and Death

For the early women settlers in the colony and for those who founded families here and became the citizens of South Australia, life according to the picture given in Franc's novels was a life of work. She portrayed men and women who—like Matilda Evans and her siblings—had no option but to disregard their previous position in society and undertake work which in England would have greatly reduced their social standing. Her characters (unlike those of her sister Emily in *Colonial Pen-Scratchings* who feel themselves degraded and suffer accordingly) show no signs of believing themselves demeaned by these necessary activities. If they are 'ladies' and 'gentlemen' by birth and upbringing they retain their belief in themselves and accept that they will regain their social standing once they have made their way in the world.

Many of her women are thrown on their own resources or work with their brothers to make a living. Teaching was the obvious means for gently-born female immigrants in financial trouble, but labouring on a farm might be necessary, at least at first. Plain sewing and dressmaking were also possibilities. Nettie Alton in *'Two Sides to Every Question'* owned a Wheeler and Wilson sewing machine, which after the sudden death of her farmer father and the transfer of herself, her invalid mother and her young brother Tom to a back street of Adelaide, became not only the chief source of their income but also their 'handsomest piece of furniture'. Later after a move to a better district she was able to take in Arthur Delta as a lodger as well.

Lizzie and Edie Wallace of *Golden Gifts* uncomplainingly did the rough work of their little farm for a considerable period after their arrival in South Australia: when they could afford a servant they were happy to give up the backbreaking washing but continued to work hard. Seventeen-year-old Katie, newly keeping house for her brothers, was constantly at work and soon defeated the prognostications of the local gossip.

> 'Seen her? yes, flying past like a race-horse or a shooting star, just a flash of blue, and then she was gone.' And Mrs Bateman's vixen eyes gave an additional twinkle as memory restored that flying figure. 'That's all I've seen, and all I am likely to see, I warrant,' she continued. 'No more butter or cheese either from Sunny Hollow now, I reckon. Feathers and the churnwork won't agree, depend upon it. I'm sorry, too, for those are fine cows of Fred Linwood's, and they do give nice butter.'
>
> *Vermont Vale*, p. 61

The 'delinquent Katie' turned up almost immediately with a basket on her arm containing 'rolls of the purest butter in any number'.

Older well-bred women might go as housekeepers to the houses of those who had money, perhaps more money than morals. 'Sensitive and proud' Mrs Benson, a widow 'accustomed in other days to good society, and familiar with the felicities which wealth alone can bestow', worked in uncongenial circumstances as a housekeeper for rich Mrs Norton in *The Master of Ralston*. She remained with her upstart mistress only because she loved the family's country home.

Some widows took in boarders. Louis Conway's landlady in Margaret Street, Mrs Layton, was 'long past middle age, small of stature, thin, almost to emaciation of form, but every inch a lady, in spite of a meagre purse and uncongenial work and surroundings' (*Silken Cords*). She was rewarded at the end by the death of distant relative who left her a competency in England. Arthur Delta's first landlady on the other hand was not a lady. She was a superficially fascinating Irish woman with three daughters avid for husbands. Arthur was attracted by the advertisement for 'a home in a private family, where only two or three gentlemen were accommodated, with the use of a piano' but his life there had very little privacy. The husband, Mr Delaney, was a drunkard and a burden to his family. He later died after being found 'lying near the banks of the Torrens, half dead, from the excessive use of alcohol and the subsequent exposure'. But like Mrs Layton Mrs Delaney was finally rewarded for her efforts—'Old Uncle Floarty's dead at last and has left ever so much money to ma!' Matilda gave credit to Mrs Delaney for her determination to make a respectable living for her husband and daughters (*Two Sides*).

Tough Mrs Bateman, another working woman who was not a lady, kept the local store with the help of her daughter. Although she is something of a comic character her situation is treated with sympathy.

> Mrs Bateman was a widow—a widow with two daughters the very counterpart of herself. The loss of her husband was rather gain to her, for during his life he kept her poor; while freed from what she never scrupled to call an incumbrance, she had boldly started on her own track, and prospered.
>
> *Vermont Vale*, p. 54

In *Silken Cords* Maude and Conny Clyde surprisingly went with their brother Edward to the goldfields in spite of his strong disapproval, and showed themselves highly capable. They ignored the ridicule and warnings of their friends, took up their places on the goldfields, kept the tents clean and attractive, cooked for the party and fossicked for themselves. They accumulated a 'neat little secret hoard of our own' and in the end considered themselves 'very well dowered'. Edward admitted that his sisters had far more energy than he had.

Organising, cleaning, cooking, milking, working in the dairy, looking after the fowls, gardening, jam-making, preserving, making and mending the clothes of the household, rug-making, knitting—there was plenty to keep these pioneer women occupied, especially when they themselves might need to take the produce to stores or markets where it could be sold. The wives of Matilda's established farmers also worked hard even when their comparative affluence and position in society made it not only unnecessary but socially even perhaps a little demeaning. They prided themselves on their usefulness to their families. Mrs Ralston, mother of wealthy forty-year-old Bennett Ralston, who had no need to do anything but supervise, still worked in the dairy, still rolled up her sleeves and put on an apron to help with the preserving, and when Bennett was absent in Adelaide rode round the property on a 'quiet old mare' making sure that the farm work went on smoothly.

Only rich women did not work. The inhabitants of many of the 'big houses' are portrayed as idle, unsatisfied girls and women, wasting their time reading sensational novels with 'ominous yellow covers' and caring for no-one but themselves. Elsie Clinton in *Two Sides* was too lazy even to help with the sewing for her own wedding. These idle women were usually Anglicans, lack-lustre adherents to a religion which Matilda saw as dependent on 'forms' and not on commitment and belief. Her later novels show some easing of this extreme position, but it is always clear that she believed that Anglicans tended to be social rather than real Christians. They relied on formal church services and not on the words of the Bible.

Thurza Kingsley of *Golden Gifts* had more spirit than most of the rich daughters in Matilda's novels, although she had been 'spoilt from her very infancy'. Matilda paints a picture of a young woman waiting to find a purpose in life.

> Perhaps Thurza's life was monotonous. She said it was and wearied sadly of it, though fortune had been lavish in its bestowals upon her. Her father was a thriving Adelaide mer-chant, and his son Godfrey bid fair to follow in his footsteps. Every morning therefore witnessed their departure for the metropolis, and for the remainder of the day her world was comprised in the beauty of the Glen Osmond neighbourhood, casual visitors, her dear but quiet aunt, Mrs Dunstan, the maids, her birds, and flowers. Music ought certainly not to be forgotten, but she often wearied of that; she could not play for ever, she said, with no one to listen or appreciate. Needlework, plain or fancy, she voted a bore. She tried her hand at model-ling wax flowers, but her impatient fingers cracked the wax, and destroyed the petals as fast as she made them. She rode out sometimes with her aunt, but her aunt's driving did not suit her mercurial nature; and on no account on such occasions were the reins entrusted to her hands.
>
> *Golden Gifts*, p. 84

Thurza soon learned to admire the energy and Christianity of the hardworking Wallaces and was willing to join them in a life of effort even before her father's ruin and sudden death made it inevitable. Martin Wallace and his sisters had not lost caste in their own eyes in this new society, even though Martin was a market gardener who took his own produce to market. *Golden Gifts* clearly shows that for Matilda fulfilment was to be found in commitment to Christian values and hard work, and not in wealth, although it is also clear in this and other novels that wealth will be welcomed if it is an accompaniment to work and not merely a release from it.

Depasquale found that Matilda's novels stressed order 'to an obsessive degree'. He quoted a passage from *Minnie's Mission* which describes the beautifully ordered gardens and outhouses of a wealthy country landowner. All the big houses with their lovely gardens in Franc's books are described in a similar way. Contemporary accounts suggest that in the case of the wealthy she was merely describing what everyone could see—and it is only to be expected that successful colonists should be proud that their efforts had resulted in the triumph of man over nature.

But the same desire for order is felt by all the characters to whom Matilda is sympathetic, no matter how poor they are. For her no doubt the well-ordered household reflected the well-ordered soul. She describes in loving detail the interiors of cottages, suggesting the efforts her characters have made to furnish their rooms prettily and to keep them neat and tidy.

> The little room was very pleasant that afternoon, so perfectly neat and spotless. The chimney, not of quite so large dimensions as many of its neighbours, was filled with fresh flowers and waving grasses, for the little kettle was boiling in a tiny shed outside that usually did service as a kitchen. The door and window stood wide open, giving a full view of everything green and lovely without, while the perfume of the garden flowers wandered in with every breeze. A few of the best of them were nestled together in a vase upon the table, and presently, to keep them company, Annie placed there a little, old-fashioned, oval tray, and upon this some of that quaint, rich, old china, that does one's heart good to see; rich and deep in colour, but not ancient in make, though not, perhaps, of the

orthodox bush dimensions, or calculated to satisfy all colonial thirst. These, and the silver tea-pot and cream-jug and spoons, were relics of past days of affluence, some of the few things saved out of a vast sacrifice of household treasures.

Vermont Vale, p. 113

There are many such passages in these novels and it is easy to dismiss them as repetitive and trite. Margaret Allen has suggested that running through the work of Maud Jeanne Franc is 'the fundamental element of domestic ideology, namely the idea that the home is woman's sphere, where she must keep everything running smoothly for the ease and comfort of her husband, the breadwinner'.

This is indisputable, but it seems to me that for Matilda there was in addition a very strong emotional commitment to the well-ordered, poorly furnished, but welcoming and attractive domestic interior. It was one of the things she most enjoyed writing about. It was the interior itself and not the fact that the husband and father would return to it which concerned her. In the case of the interior described above there was no man to return at night, and schoolmistress Annie was the breadwinner.

For Matilda describing interiors such as this one where the scanty belongings of the present were combined with a few treasures from the past enabled her to reconcile her two lives, her memories of a past comfortable life in England and the stark reality of her life in Australia which for twenty years at least and probably for thirty was a continuing struggle. In life creating such interiors was a woman's work and helped to give her life value. For many of Matilda's female characters decorating such rooms was in addition one of their forms of play. There was little else open to them.

> ... the little room opened immediately from the door; there was no formality of a passage or hall between.
>
> A plain little room, plain as plain could well be. A few simple chairs of unpolished cedar, colonial cedar and of colonial make, which in those days was not particularly artistic, a sofa and a table of the same. White matting on the floor, and one or two heavy cloth rugs of home knitting and manufacture on the hearth and elsewhere. And yet there was an air of refinement

about the whole, due partly to the arrangement of things, due a great deal to the small cottage piano, with its crimson silk front gleaming through a large, handsome antimacassar of darned netting, which was thrown over it—due also to the beautiful crayon drawings of heads and landscapes hanging round the room, here and there interspersed by a group of flowers in water-colours, and all cheaply but prettily bordered by frames of mingled shells and sea-weed, or pine-cones, skilfully arranged and varnished over, the cheapest and most unpretending materials,—all, too, of home manufacture.

The late master had left a few shelves on either side the fireplace, and these had been added to in number and nearly reached the ceiling, and were filled with books. Two small crystal vases stood on the mantle-piece, filled with ferns, a neat little clock ticked musically between them, and in the corner of the room, in the centre of a small round table which was covered by a dark-blue cloth, stood another home contrivance, a sort of double saucer, one above the other, but so crowded with roses and jessamine that the simplicity and crudeness of the arrangement was a mystery known only to the constructor.

The Master of Ralston, p. 34

I feel Matilda's pleasure in what she is describing though I cannot admire her pedestrian style nor the artifacts—fashionable then no doubt, but thankfully no longer so. The passage does give a good indication of what many of her young women did with their spare time. Of course they also paid visits—very time-consuming for most people who had no means of transport except walking—and when they had means they helped the poor.

Of the many leisure activities of which accounts can be found in contemporary newspapers—horse-racing, pigeon-racing, cricket, boating, local shows and ploughing contests—none appear in these novels. I have gained the impression that Matilda's life had been so circumscribed by her responsibilities that she knew little of such entertainments. There are a few dances mentioned, very much disapproved of in the early novels, but tolerated as time went on. The city dwellers in *John's Wife* attended a Flower Show and 'an interesting lecture on Music, with illustrations'. But few such activities are mentioned.

The detailed domestic interiors help us to understand what in Matilda's limited experience women might do in their spare time.

For her men there was little except work unless they were bad or weak in which case they gambled and drank. There are public houses detracting from the health of all the little communities she describes. But good men stayed at home and sat with their wives or mothers in the evenings and perhaps read to them. Some who were struggling to make a living did piece-work—engrossing— from lawyers' offices. Martin Wallace prepared and gave a lecture in Adelaide on horticulture which was well-attended by both men and women, in fact it was a major outing and entertainment.

In Amber Vale, the township of *The Master of Ralston*, the Institute Library room became the centre of activities for many of the young people of the district. They formed a group to raise money for a new building, gave a concert and organised a bazaar. There is a strong sense of community in this novel and of lively life for young people. This was Matilda's last novel, possibly written in ill health, but it suggests that the writer was now able to take a broader and more benign view of society.

But mostly in Matilda's novels leisure activities are centred in the life of the church or chapel. At services, choir practice, prayer meetings, tea meetings—these are the places where good people are shown meeting together and living a social life. If there was no chapel building near, services might be held in a private house as happened at the Wallaces' in *Golden Gifts*. Neighbours soon began attending these services.

One of the most interesting examples of a religious service as a leisure activity occurs in *Vermont Vale* after the death of the Ranger baby from dysentery (the disease which had killed the first child of Ephraim, Matilda's husband). There was 'no regular graveyard at Vermont, no enclosed place for the dead' and so the baby's father had dug a grave at the bottom of their own garden. Katie Linwood and Annie Maitland and two other young women all dressed in white were pall-bearers. A 'bevy of young people of either sex' travelled to the burial service in a waggon, 'their merriment only half kept down by the remembrance of the cause of the gathering'. They flirted with each other and gave vent to their happiness by singing—they sang hymns of course because that was what they knew—and could barely control their bubbling spirits. Only after they met the pastor did they begin to quieten, and then 'a little sense of outward decorum, and the near approach to the scene of death, quieted the most reckless and giddy among them'. The service is described at length and almost all were moved to tears, but Katie returned alone, unable to endure 'the babble of nonsense' which would be her fate on the waggon.

No comment was made by the narrator on the behaviour of this 'bevy of young people'. It is clear that they were curious and interested, and that they were moved by the drama they were watching, but it was an outing to them, a kind of entertainment. To Matilda such an outing was preferable to the party and dance which the local doctor had given earlier for his daughter. It gives us a curious insight into Matilda's world.

There are many deaths in Matilda's novels, although there are no other funeral services. Almost half the babies born in South Australia during her early years of writing died in childhood and so it is not surprising that there are so many deaths of children in her stories or that she used these deaths for special purposes. The death of the Ranger baby helped Katie to think more seriously about Christianity because she had known and loved the child and she found the death very hard to accept. But it was not only Katie with whom Matilda was concerned. She was clearly attempting in this story to comfort those grieving over the loss of children and to reconcile them to what she saw as God's choice.

In other novels in a clear use of her own experience she shows women dying of consumption as her own mother had done—Julie in *Marian*, Lilian Spencer in *Emily's Choice*, Nellie Macdonald in *Silken Cords*, Lena in *No Longer a Child*—or in the case of Minnie in *Minnie's Mission* of congestion of the lungs (pneumonia) as Ephraim's first wife had done. Men too die in ways she had observed. They die suddenly of heart disease or stroke as her father and her husband had done—Beattie's father in *Beatrice Melton's Discipline*, Captain Macdonald in *Silken Cords*, Percy Norton in *The Master of Ralston*. There are other deaths as well, notably from alcoholism or complications following accidents caused by drunkenness.

It was not a morbid attitude to life which caused writers like

Matilda to write detailed death scenes. Nor are these descriptions sentimental in the sense that they are charged with false emotion. Such writers are sometimes accused of glossing over horrors and overdoing the sweet cheerfulness and Christian tranquillity with which sufferers, particularly those with consumption, meet death. Matilda makes no attempt to disguise the horrors of consumption; she merely does not dwell on them.

> Sometimes Marian thought home was the best place for her [Julie]. She feared that terribly quiet, hot, tormenting cough. She feared that white brow, the blue veins of which were more than ever visible. She feared the etherialized attenuated figure.
> *Marian*, p. 316

> Poor Lily!—a veritable lily now, drooping on its stem, the crimson welling from her lips, all else so colourless.
> *Emily's Choice*, p. 185

The deaths of Julie Burton and Lilian Spencer are certainly dwelt upon at length; both have struggled against the disease until they die exhausted, and both have been helped to accept their fate with Christian resignation. But their deaths are no more tranquil and devout than the death of Matilda's own mother as she described it in a letter to her half-brother George:

> I never quitted her for weeks, day or night, till towards the last, when the surgeon insisted upon it, and then alternately we watched by her side. Truly, oh truly, she slept in Jesus. So sweet a sleep, we scarcely knew when the last sigh was drawn. Firmly she relied upon the Stronghold for refuge. 'He is a Stronghold, I feel it,' my dear patient mother exclaimed one day. I cannot say more in this letter; you know how truly our dear mother walked out the Christian, lived on Christ; ah, and died leaning on his bosom.

The language has dated, but Matilda's sincerity must be accepted. Tompkins in *Sensational Designs* has shown how such death-bed scenes may be viewed differently by observers with different expectations. For people of Matilda's beliefs physical suffering at this time was so unimportant as not to be worth recording. Dying 'in sin' was what was to be dreaded. That people could die reconciled and happy, could 'fall asleep in Jesus', was a matter of rejoicing. Many of Matilda's readers would have shared her expectations and she would have hoped that those who did not would have been led by her many death-bed scenes to think seriously about their own future after death. She often points out that those who put off the serious consideration of religion for some later day may be overtaken by death before they expect it.

Death plays a very important part in Matilda's novels. Attitudes to work, sex, marriage and the family—'A bad home's better than none at all, to my thinking,' says Ben Hall of *Hall's Vineyard*—are all very important but it is in their attitudes to death that the depth of the characters' religious convictions can be discerned.

The deaths of people in and before their prime were very common at the time at which Matilda was writing. People today expect to live to be old—even though not all these expectations are realised. But Matilda's readers lived with the knowledge that the untimely death of some of those they loved was inevitable. One of the functions of her novels was to prepare them for such death and to help them endure their loss. She wished to make them aware that their own hold on life was fragile and to show them how to prepare for what might lie ahead.

CHAPTER 12

School-house and Schoolroom

Not one of Matilda's stories mentions a writer, although writing was one of the avenues which women in difficult circumstances in England often pursued and was a choice she had made herself. Perhaps she saw the openings for colonial women as being extremely limited. Perhaps for her it was an experience too private or too traumatic to write about. It is surprising because her other way of earning money, through teaching, is a constant subject.

Seven of her novels and a number of her short stories deal with teaching in some detail. It is hard to deduce much about her own practice as a teacher since she gives pictures of so many different situations, but much about the satisfactions and problems of teaching at that time can be discovered. It is hard not to see the following passage, unexpected in context and irrelevant to the story, as giving Matilda's own deeply-felt response.

> As Katie crept under the fence in sight of the school-house the door opened widely, and one after another, in wild delight at freedom, rushed forth the happy children, some one way, some another. School was out, and there was no longer any necessity to restrain the laugh and shout, no longer need to keep quiet the restless feet that would sometimes rebel against all law and rule, impatient for a run. Books, and slates, and maps, farewell to you till Monday. Respite now for the pale, weary teacher. Respite now for the almost as weary little ones. Hurrah for the holiday for both! Precious boon this Saturday and Sunday to the teacher and the taught!
>
> *Vermont Vale*, p. 110

I warm to the writer who sympathises so impartially with teacher and taught!

The experiences of Miss Congreve and Mrs Evans who ran so many different schools and different types of schools in South Australia has enriched the novels of Maud Jeanne Franc and given us many glimpses into a particular area of life which is being increasingly researched. These fictional portraits can help flesh out the material discovered in records and newspapers.

Although Matilda herself conducted several schools in the city it was chiefly country schools of which she wrote. Only *John's Wife* gives a glimpse of a city school, and that is not a licensed school. Milly and Ellie Ashwin took a few pupils in their own home—day pupils only—to 'eke out our slender means'. This would not have been a licensed school and Milly could not have made very much money at all, since she would have received no Board of Education stipend. Even so the school became a necessity, emotionally as well as financially, when Ellie and John married and Milly was left to fend for herself. Milly was not really an enthusiastic teacher.

> I am teaching steadily still; and provided I have docile and moderately intelligent scholars, *that* is no hardship. The difficulty is to find such. Parents may choose teachers for their children; but, alas! teachers cannot select their pupils. They must take capacities as they come, good, bad, or indifferent; receiving the same payment for a dull as for a bright pupil. Of course I mean *money* payment; for one now and then encounters pupils who more than repay all the attention lavished on them. No, teaching itself is no hardship; and on the whole, perhaps, I have less to complain of unrequited labours than many of the weary, tired, worn-out teachers of this colony.
>
> *John's Wife*, p. 147.

I suspect that this attitude was not unlike Matilda's. She was a successful teacher, found the occupation rewarding and knew that she had little to complain about. But just as Milly was rescued from teaching by marriage so was Matilda, and the novel giving the picture of her most reluctant teacher, Emily Owen, was that which followed her husband's death and her own forced return to teaching. It seems likely that Matilda was a competent and conscientious teacher rather than a delighted one, although she does give glimpses of 'born teachers' in some of her stories.

A teacher of many years' experience myself, I have looked in vain for the kind of comment which would show that Matilda herself found teaching an absorbing and fulfilling occupation. I suspect that she was an energetic, capable and compassionate rather than a dedicated teacher, and a highly competent school administrator who liked the family atmosphere of boarding schools.

She was only thirty when she first advertised at Mount Barker offering 'a happy home and a careful education' to young boarders. After her husband's death she ran private boarding schools in her own home and I suspect that that is what she enjoyed, for when she moved to Adelaide in 1869 she did not take the option of once again becoming a licensed Board of Education teacher though she surely could have done so. When in the year before her death she was anxious once again to take up teaching it was obviously of a small boarding school that she was thinking—she remarked that she could not undertake a school in the house they were living in. It was to her writing that she was truly dedicated though she clearly liked teaching as well.

Interestingly most of the schools she describes are licensed ones—Milly Ashwin and Beatrice Melton are the only teachers to take pupils into their homes. Matilda did not run a school like Milly Ashwin's, unless she took a few pupils into her first home in North Adelaide before she had mustered the required number to take out a licence. Beatrice Melton's school was like the schools Matilda ran in Angaston and in Buxton Street, North Adelaide, schools which were primarily boarding schools, though they had day pupils as well. Beattie's home was large with nine or ten rooms and a verandah all round. When the school first opened they had four boarders and a dozen day girls who came in from the surrounding farms. The girls slept four in a room, and when Kenneth Gordon's three children were added to the number little Willie slept in Beattie's room. After Willie's death and following the arrival of two more boarders, Kenneth's daughters Isabel and Annie slept in one bed in Beattie's room.

One of the rooms in the house had been turned into a large pleasant schoolroom. There was a fireplace, and two long tables around which the children sat, older ones at one table and the younger ones at the other. Beattie and her sister Katie shared the teaching duties until Katie's marriage took her away. Beattie enjoyed teaching and the picture given of the large group living in this friendly house is an attractive and tranquil one (*Beatrice Melton's Discipline*). This seems to me to be the situation which Matilda found most fulfilling.

Life in the licensed schools was not always so easy. The most vivid picture is given in *Vermont Vale*. The schoolhouse, we are told, was a 'rude slab hut'; it was in fact a tiny dwelling. The front door, over which there was a small porch, opened into the small central sitting room. Out of this opened on one side the 'neat' bedroom, on the other the schoolroom. That was all. There was a tiny shed outside which was used as a kitchen. This was perhaps not so very different from the three-roomed house in Finniss Street, North Adelaide where Matilda had her first school, or from her school-houses at Yunkunga and Mount Barker. The schoolroom furniture was minimal.

> Well-worn forms of the rudest material and most primitive make, of red gum, time-polished into a hue almost rivalling mahogany; long narrow tables, by no means remarkably level, of the same material, and supported by heavy blocks driven into the floor, did service as desks; two or three maps hung suspended from the roughly-plastered, lime-washed walls, and a long shelf, from one side of the wall-plate to the other, held books and slates innumerable, only to be reached by climbing on the table.
>
> *Vermont Vale*, p. 69

Annie Maitland, the schoolmistress of *Vermont Vale* who 'in a weary desponding mood' confided her troubles to Fred Linwood, helps us to understand the problems country teachers faced.

> Two or three things had troubled me. Unkindness from the parents of one of my pupils, unjust complaints of non-improvement, though the child was sent but half the time, and the hard and unkind manner in which the complaint was made, from

one who professed to belong to the same heavenly Father, who profess to obey the injunction 'love as brethren,' in the first place grieved me, for it was cruel, and the mischief they have tried to do me worse still. Yet, perhaps, it was silly in me to take notice of it; but then, Mr. Linwood, it is hard, very hard, after labouring with all your power among your pupils, doing all you can for their advancement, having to contend with all their carelessness and inattention, or obstinacy, to meet with so little sympathy, so little help or appreciation from the parents; though parents I need not say, for this is but a solitary case, and therefore ought not to have troubled me.

Vermont Vale, p. 262.

So might teachers speak almost 150 years later. Yet these teachers had to contend with added difficulties brought about by the great range in ages of the students and by wild variations in attendance. In *Marian* the narrator—and Matilda at the time was still teaching in her country school at Mount Barker and knew what she was talking about—complained vigorously about the cavalier attitude that even enlightened parents like the Burtons had towards education. The two absent members of the Burton family, Frank and Charlie,

were at the distant township, *getting education*; and had been doing so *right off* for six months. Poor boys! in common with other bush children, they had had little enough previously, except that which the farm afforded, and of that they had had a pretty good share. We need not say how culpable is the conduct of many parents in our adopted country, who, awarding to the schoolmaster a quarter now and a quarter then, are pleased to term this *educating their children*. Surely no better fate awaits the unfortunate tutor of these very wild *young ideas* than that inflicted, according to the heathen fable, as a severe punishment—the filling with water of a tub full of holes.

Marian, p. 23.

It is easy to sympathise with teachers who suffered from this practice of keeping children away for a quarter at a time and then sending them back later for another quarter or so when it was convenient. It is no wonder that inspectors frequently complained that standards were low.

Emily Owen was forced into teaching by parents who attended

her husband's chapel and had failed to honour their contract with him. There were two reasons for this. One was that they felt responsible for their pastor and if his wife would run a school for girls—the previous schoolmaster had just left—then they could add to his income without having to pay both pastor and school-teacher. The other was that a young schoolmaster was coming to take the boys and they did not 'fancy' placing their own 'great girls' under the tuition of an unmarried man. Emily had no objection to trying teaching—she thought she would like it. But in practice she found many difficulties. She had no ideas or enthusiasm for the job and she had to use a makeshift schoolroom in her own house while the male teacher gained the use of the detached schoolhouse. The arrival of her pupils on her first day was enough to highlight the problems.

> They came—not more than a dozen that day, but they fully occupied the time, and set Emily speculating as to what she should do when more came. The duties were new to her, and she had to conjure up memories of her own school-days to enable her in the least to arrange the order of things. Even that she found would not do entirely; the girls in most cases were backward, and difficult to arrange or classify—at any rate just at first—and the hours passed away, and three o'clock came, leaving the forlorn little teacher with spirits that were very difficult to raise sufficiently for the comfort and cheer that were needed within.
>
> *Emily's Choice*, p. 262.

It was soon obvious that Emily was not a success as a school-teacher, though she tried hard. She had a young child, a sick and very depressed husband who because he was a pastor was on the premises a great deal of the time, she was soon pregnant again herself—and she was unable to keep up her numbers.

> Emily was truly very weary: her school did not prosper as she desired it; her cares were too divided. Teaching is not every one's vocation—it was scarcely hers. At any rate, with all these anxieties so heavily weighing her down, she found it a very great trial. It seemed to her that the duties of her home, and the duties of her school, continually clashed and wrangled.
>
> p. 273

It is no wonder that she relinquished her post thankfully when Gilbert found a more congenial pastorate in Victoria. But by then she had lost her baby. This picture of a young wife trying to make a success of a school and a home I have found rather horrifying. It is obvious that Emily would have managed the school much more successfully if she had not had to expend more energy than she could spare suppressing her worries and weariness in order to provide the kind of home which she had been led to believe that a husband must have.

This is the domestic ideology at its most appalling. I hope very much that Matilda was not writing from experience in this part of her novel and that the last year or so of her husband's life was not made miserable by unhelpful parishioners as Gilbert Owen's was. And that she did not have to take on teaching while she had both a husband and the four little children to care for. Even if she did not have this added burden she knew enough to know what it would be like. Although sentimentally depicted, the situation described here seems uncomfortably real.

In spite of this, perhaps because of it, *Emily's Choice* was one of Maud Jeanne Franc's most popular novels. It may be indeed that female readers at least responded well to the picture of weak little fearful and apparently frail Emily showing so much greater strength determination and staying power than her emotionally fragile husband. It is impossible to know now whether readers and writer then saw what modern readers see—Emily being exploited by all who knew her. It may be that here we have a case of a text in which an author has subconsciously revealed her own suppressed dissatisfactions which were not obvious to her then nor to her contemporary readers.

Not all Matilda's licensed schoolteachers are women, though her men teachers tend to be unsatisfactory. Edward Owen of *Hall's Vineyard*, however, was everything a schoolmaster should be. He was good-looking, he had a 'first-rate school', a 'snug little sum in the bank', a 'nice snug little house' adjoining his school-room awaiting Jenny Semple when her father would permit them to marry, and in addition he preached total abstinence! A reader has no fear that he will leave his wife to run the school. However, the situation of husband or father evading his responsibilities and leaving his wife or daughter in charge of a school—either his or one she takes on to support the family—is a recurring theme in Matilda's work. Frail little girls are frequently the breadwinners. Edith Manville had a brutal drunken father.

> 'Her father has a school, but the greater part of the teaching falls upon his daughter, on whom also devolves all the household work; and she is a little bit of a creature, and, as you say, a sweet and lovely girl, and as good as lovely ... He is very seldom sober, and, but for Edith, would have lost the school over and over again.'
>
> *Minnie's Mission*, p. 186

Edith, like so many of Matilda's characters, was rescued by his death and her marriage.

Mr Valma in *The Master of Ralston* was a real scholar and loved his books. Bennett Ralston thought he had done a fine thing for the district when he arranged for this new schoolmaster to come to Amber Vale. We are given here a picture of a leading citizen taking upon himself to arrange matters. He met Valma (and his daughter!) in the city, believed him to be an eligible candidate for the position just vacated by the previous master and invited him to come to take over the school. The parents of the school children readily consented, especially as Bennett had made a 'very liberal contribution towards the school funds'. This was a good position for Valma. The school was in a wealthy area and there was a cottage for the family and a free standing school-house.

> The school-house in question was in reality a mere compound of logs and the customary rude mortar, but it had one advantage—it was of ample size, and had in the first instance been well built, with a good shingle roof and substantial floor, which had stood well in spite of the restless feet that for many a year had traversed it. Plastering, too, had rendered it very passable to the eye, and this was all that was considered necessary for a licensed school of the period. The fittings of the interior, in the matter of desks and benches, were of primitive workmanship and material—red gum, polished by long use and friction to almost the colour of mahogany.
>
> *The Master of Ralston*, p. 13

Unfortunately Ernest Valma was not really suited to school-teaching.

> He was, in fact, too refined for his position. A classical education is certainly not required for the simple tuition of reading, writing, and ciphering—the leading elements taught in licensed schools of our past history, and to which it would perhaps be well if our *free*[1] schools of the present day were more closely restricted. Boys fresh from the spade or the plough, with heads innocent of even the simplest rudiments of the 'three R's'; girls rough and untaught, both in first principles or manners, were certainly crude materials for the manipulations of a B.A.; and whether the children or the master got the worst of it in the effort to obtain or to teach, may clearly be a matter for speculation.
>
> *The Master of Ralston*, p. 14

It soon became obvious that Ernest Valma had little interest in anything but his books. Although there was an idle son the daughters did the bulk of the teaching in the school, and even in the holidays Netta was occupied with adding up the school accounts, preparing a report for the Board of Education, writing out new rules, and sending orders for fresh schoolbooks. 'Her father had no inclination to go to town, since he could receive his cheque through the post, and obtain his books by coach.' Netta did not find teaching easy—she took to it 'as kindly as the poor eel does the services of the fish-woman,' said Nelly Cameron. Nelly took an interest in the girls and peeped in through the schoolroom door.

> There sat Netta at her father's desk, pale as a snowdrop, and as graceful, bending over a heap of slates, the errors of which she was marking and again passing to the class to whom she had just been dictating, a class composed of varied elements—big boys and girls almost as big, some indeed bigger than their young teacher ... The sound of little voices chanting the mul-

---

1. Matilda may mean some comment on the 1875 Education Act here. She could not be referring to free elementary education, because that did not come in until after her death. But with the introduction in 1875 of compulsory elementary education and a prescribed curriculum the whole focus of education changed. It seems she did not approve.

tiplication table directed her attention to another pretty scene. Rosie—bright, sparkling, mirthful Rosie—in the midst of a smiling group of little ones, all eagerly following her lead, all catching the sunny brightness of her smile, till the table with its intricacies seemed a mere pastime invented for their pleasure.

The Master of Ralston, p. 253

Nelly thought they must both be born teachers 'or they could never stand all this routine, and make it pleasant to the taught'. But only Rosie seemed to be enjoying herself. Nelly accidentally interrupted their activities with a result that school was immediately over—not quite what might have been expected from those old days of supposedly strict discipline.

She moved a step nearer, but at that moment the bright eyes of one of the little ones had spied her out, and with a merry laugh and pointing finger betrayed her.

It was all at an end now, the lesson and the discipline, and there was nothing for it but to give the order for dismissal. Then came the clamour of war, the rapid putting up slates and books, the packing of satchels, and the final seizure of hats and bonnets, and filing out, with due reverence scarcely sustained, and the merry shout and laugh barely held in till the open air was gained, and the release, ten minutes earlier than usual, was fully realized.

p. 253

It was lucky for Rosie that the Valmas came into a legacy, otherwise on Netta's marriage she would have had to run the school by herself.

Another delinquent father was Dr Harden ('Dr. Harden's Theories' in *The Chronicle*, 25 December 1886) who abandoned his lucrative medical practice in favour of farming on strictly scientific lines, unfortunately without the necessary capital. When ruin loomed his daughter Mada undertook 'to be the provider' by taking over a vacant school a mile away. This little school in a bare dusty area was the sort of school often to be found in the country—'a wooden structure, along the front of which was stretched a rude but broad verandah'.

There was nothing striking in the appearance of this structure. It was simply one of the old primitive schoolhouses, put up by

> the united efforts of some of the male members of the several
> families at little expense beyond that of time and labour, and
> some of these males, though they acknowledged the necessity
> for the culture of their young ones, grudged not a little this
> disposal of their time, and would have been better pleased, as
> many are in the present time, if Government had kindly
> stepped in and saved them the trouble.

Maybe this was the kind of building which Mr Walter Paterson
had had erected for Matilda at Yunkunga. It was a building which
had more than one function and the scholars themselves kept it in
order.

> The windows were wide open—so was the door, but there was
> little to be seen besides clouds of dust that were evidently in
> process of being swept up by two stout maidens, whose turn it
> doubtless was to perform this office and assist in clearing the
> room, for it was the end of the week, and everything was
> required to be in perfect order for the Sabbath-school and an
> afternoon service which was regularly held there every Sunday.

When the sweeping was finished and the girls had tidied the
room and locked up the books Mada closed the windows—'all but
a narrow strip at the top of each'—and locked the door behind
her. She pulled on her long gloves, then 'elevating her parasol
and swinging her lunch and workbasket on her arm' set off with
her young sister and brother to walk home. (They are all picked
up by her lover in his buggy.) By the end of the story Dr Harden
had been persuaded to return to the practice of medicine and his
daughter, another incipient sacrifice to a male idiosyncrasy, had
been set free to marry.

'Tom Morison's Golden Christmas' (*The Chronicle*, 23 December 1882) presents a similar situation. When after their arrival in
Adelaide Mr Morison could not find work for himself or his son
he bought a small property in the country and attempted to farm.
He soon

> appropriated one of the six small rooms as his study. He was
> engaged in writing lectures which were to be successfully given
> in the future. It kept him amused and occupied during the
> months of waiting, at any rate ['it will be months before we can

plough or sow—still longer before we can reap'], and made him feel he was doing something, though Tom privately gave it as his opinion that the subjects he had chosen were not likely to be popular in Australia.

Needless to say it was daughter Ray who found a job. She was asked to open a school about a mile away which she did with 'complete success'. The neighbourhood was not a large one and she had only twenty pupils, but 'the boys and girls, rough and untaught as they were, soon learnt to respect their young teacher, and not a few to love her'. Ray rose at six to work at home before she set out, still fresh and eager, 'swinging her little luncheon basket in her hand, and spreading her large white sunshade with its green lining' to undertake her four to five hours teaching. Meanwhile her brother Tom studied geology and then sought for and found enough gold to rescue the family fortunes. (Such finds in South Australia were rare but not unprecedented.)

It is not surprising that with her own history of supporting others Matilda should return again and again to this theme. Some of her young women visibly wilt under their responsibilities, although no-one gives up. Others like Mada Harden and Ray Morison are determined and cheerful. Teaching is not a major part of any of her stories, although the examples I have presented may give this impression. But it is often there in the background, enabling present-day readers to glimpse what it was like to teach in schools in those days and also to understand how deeply Matilda felt for the many women in the colony who through death or disaster or male fecklessness were thrown on their own resources and took on this particular task, one for which they may or may not have been suited. She emphasises their physical smallness and frailty—maybe she was small herself, or maybe this was her crude method of bidding for the reader's sympathy—but they are all uncomplaining and great-hearted.

They do not criticise their menfolk, but it must have been a very insensitive reader who did not note that in Matilda's stories the women are on the whole more reliable than the men. It is not difficult to imagine that we are seeing in the hero of her last novel, that paragon of virtue Bennett Ralston, who is so very good to his mother, Matilda's fictional attempt to provide herself with the completely reliable masculine support which had escaped her in life. Her portrait of Mrs Ralston is revealing. Needing no sympathy from the reader she is 'tall and fine-looking' and is full of confidence and trust in her son. Their relationship is a major interest in the novel; Bennett's choice of a wife a major concern. This was a new theme for Matilda.

When she was writing this novel her own sons were in their early twenties. Sadly she did not live to discover whether they would have provided the loving support that this last novel suggests that she longed for. But perhaps their vigorous opposition when at the age of fifty-seven she wished once again to take up teaching gave her in one way at least a very deep satisfaction.

CHAPTER 13

Side-Saddles, Spring-Carts and Stylish Buggies

The world in which Matilda set her novels and stories was almost always the world of her first years in the colony. Though she refers from time to time to contemporary happenings her characters usually live in earlier times. Railways are scarcely mentioned. The railway from Adelaide to Port Adelaide was opened in 1856, and that to Gawler in 1857, but railways did not reach Angaston or Mount Barker until after the times about which she wrote. Even her last novel *The Master of Ralston*, published at the end of 1885 in the year before her death, is set much earlier, well before the 1875 Education Act about which she expressed her disapproval. Matilda's world was a world in which people walked or used horses. To a late twentieth-century reader this is one of the most interesting aspects of her work. Learning how people moved from place to place helps us to understand the pace and range of their lives.

In the 1850s rows of bullock-drays, the earliest form of conveyance, stood in the city streets. It was by bullock-dray that goods as well as people were moved about the colony. Seventeen-year-old Katie Linwood's journey to Vermont Vale to keep house for her brother gives an idea of the speed and discomfort of such travel.

> A ride on horseback, a wild scamper among the brushwood, creeks to leap, rocks to climb, anything rather than the eternal rumble of the old dray-wheels, and creeping, idle movements of the stupid bullocks, so thought Katie, but not so her father;

146

at any rate he willed otherwise. So pretty little Hebe, the pony he had given her for a birthday present, was despatched by other roads the day before, and Katie was obliged most unwillingly to submit with the best grace she could. Perched up amid sundry articles of furniture of which her brother's house was innocent, she sat martyr-like, when sit she must, through sheer fatigue. The rest of the time she was off on the wing concealed from view by the tea-tree bushes, or wattle, or anything indeed that could come between her and the old jumbling, jolting vehicle, to whose tender mercies she resigned the more patient, the more easily-accommodated Dolly, who preferred any mode of carriage to the marrow-bone stage.

Vermont Vale, p. 36

To Matilda a ride in a bullock-dray, 'a genuine rough-and-tumble ride up hill and down dale, through dust, and mud, and quagmire' was an essential colonial experience. Readers who have 'escaped' such an journey, 'be [they] who they may, let me tell them they have missed some of the real experience of bush-life, some of the positive form of bush-travelling, and must not think of professing colonial knowledge'.

In the city many people walked to work even if they had other means of transport, often over 'deeply-indented ruts, fitted only for the entrapment of unwary feet'. Louis Conway (*Silken Cords*), who was poor and had no option, always walked home to Margaret Street in North Adelaide from his job in the city, known then as South Adelaide, by the ford or by 'the narrow footbridge that spanned the lofty banks of the river', the Torrens which was—however polluted—for many years the chief source of water for the colony. This was in the 1850s when the great old red gums were still standing, before the parklands were fenced and before the City Bridge was built.

But even then there was some public transport which might be used by poor and well-to-do alike. It was a surprise to me that in the early 1850s there were 'omnibuses' and 'cars' which carried passengers from the nearer suburbs to the city. I have not been able to find a description of an Adelaide omnibus, but in England in the 1850s an omnibus was a 'four-wheeled public vehicle for carrying passengers, usually covered and frequently with seats on the roof as well as inside, plying on a fixed route'. A 'car' seems to have been a similar kind of conveyance. Marian's cousin William Greville waited on the verandah in the morning for the omnibus to come by and Marian herself, intending to shop in the 'metropolis', caught the next omnibus. She hired a cart to carry home the carpet and couch she had bought, but she herself came back in 'a comfortable corner of a return conveyance' (*Marian*).

At about the same time Andy Macdonald and Louis Conway, who might have walked home to Andy's from the city if Louis had not been so tired, secured the last two places on 'the solitary homeward car' (*Silken Cords*). After a visit with her family and friends to a crowded evening Flower Show at 'White's rooms' Milly Ashwin was glad to sink into 'the darkened shadow of the car's dingy corner' when they had caught the 'car' to return home (*John's Wife*). Herbert Turner usually walked to work on fine mornings but when late he 'hailed a passing car, and took his place in it for town' (*Little Mercy*).

Business men owned horses which might be lent to employees who had messages to deliver or business to transact out of town. Arthur Delta, an unsatisfactory employee, stole a visit to his cousin Elsie Clinton when sent with a message to a house half a mile away from her home—and stayed to lunch (*Two Sides*).

These are city scenes, but most of Matilda's stories are set in the country. In the country horses were were almost a necessity. The social standing of Matilda's characters can be gauged from the fact that most have at least access to horses, even if like Gilbert Owen, Emily's pastor husband, they had to groom them themselves (*Emily's Choice*). The difficulties of the 'poor and proud' Valma family were made obvious by the fact that Frank, the weak, lazy, unsatisfactory son, had no horse. He was easily influenced by those who would provide transport. Although he disliked Bennett Ralston, when he heard that the boy sent to him with a message from Bennett had 'brought an extra horse', he 'sprang from his bed with sudden animation'. Frank soon fell under the bad influence of Alton Norton, who took him driving round the countryside in his buggy (*The Master of Ralston*). (Needless to say Frank is one of those characters who ultimately return to England having proved a failure here.)

Farmer Burton however, a substantial landowner, collecting Marian in Adelaide and taking her through the hills to the 'farmstead fifty miles up the country', travelled with a dray which held purchases and the new Irish servant, and three riding horses, one each for himself and his son Alf, and one with a 'new side-saddle' for Marian. Marian, who had not seen a farm before even in England, knew how to ride, for the little party 'cantered off', but their late arrival at the farmstead was thought by the family to be 'sure proof' that Mr Burton had some one with him 'not accustomed to long journeys on horseback'. However they did not own a gig (a light two-wheeled one-horse carriage) and needed to borrow one for the tubercular Julie's transport to Glenelg where it was hoped she would regain her health. But the Burtons were on the way up socially, and Allen had been commissioned by his father to procure 'a pretty new conveyance of our own' by the time she was ready to return (*Marian*).

Minnie of *Minnie's Mission* was taught to ride soon after her arrival. Her cousin John made the point: 'Minnie, if you want to get about much, or see much in the country, you must positively learn to ride.' It is not long before she is independent of assistance or chaperonage. Katie Linwood (*Vermont Vale*) has her pony Hebe and rides out frequently by herself.

Winnifred Aland of *Golden Gifts* is the best horsewoman in Matilda's novels. She learned to ride as a child on a station, and unlike other women characters did not always ride side-saddle. She could ride bare-back with only a rope for bridle, she could ride with bare feet standing upon a horse's back, and she rode an unbroken horse for help after it had thrown her father and injured him—'it never needed any further breaking-in, it was as quiet as a lamb after that'.

When at the age of sixteen she was staying with her aunt in the Adelaide hills and was unhappily in love with her cousin she took her horse and rode alone for three days until she reached her father's station. Interestingly she is never criticised or condemned by the narrator for what was certainly unconventional behaviour. But Winnie did make her young step-sister promise that she would never ride without saddle and bridle: 'in the first place, it is unlady-like, and, in the second, very dangerous to those who have not learnt it very young indeed'. It has seemed to me that Matilda, although she acknowledged that Winnie would never be able to take her place in polite society if she continued to behave so wildly and unconventionally, had considerable sympathy for her strength of character, her independent attitude and her determination.

Horses were used to draw all sorts of vehicles and the present financial standing of their owners could be determined by what they drew. The hard-working German settlers drove in brightly-painted waggons, the struggling English and Scottish immigrants in drays, strong low carts without fixed sides used for carrying heavy loads. As their finances improved they might be lucky enough to afford spring-carts, light two-wheeled vehicles with springs. Some families owned carriages drawn by two or more horses, which took several people and were comfortable and elegant. Traps or buggies, light two-wheeled carriages drawn by one or two horses, were the province of the smart and the wealthy. Bennett Ralston sent his buggy for the Valma girls to come to tea with his mother:

> How pretty it was, buggy and ponies; everything so complete, so good, with the light flexible springs, soft cushions, and handsome carriage-rug. The hood was thrown quite back, that all the benefit of the balmy air, and all the beauty of the scenery might be enjoyed.
>
> *The Master of Ralston*, p. 78

A bullock-dray nearly sent them through the fence to the gully below, but only the driver realised the danger and so the girls were not disturbed. Alton Norton riding past with his sister Blanche recognised 'Ralston's turn-out' and envied him the girls. Later, driving Netta Valma, Bennett narrowly averted death at the same dangerous spot when a thunderstorm had terrified the horse. This escape and the heightened emotion it provoked brought him at last to the point of proposing.

Buggies and carriages however were expensive. John Ashwin 'set up a carriage' on his marriage—his father-in-law gave him the vehicle and 'a pair of pretty ponies' as a wedding present. But this 'very handsome gift' presented problems for a lawyer just establishing himself. As his sister Milly thought to herself: 'The carriage consumes nothing, but the ponies will; and then there must be a man employed to look after them' (*John's Wife*).

Honeymoon tours to places like Port Elliot and 'The Gulwa' (now Goolwa) were taken in buggies and carriages, and honeymoon picnics were made more comfortable when the couple could sit 'under the shade of the carriage-rug, spread, tent-like, over the shafts, while the tethered horses cropped the herbage near' (*Little Mercy*).

These times, so different from ours, are like ours too. Accidents were frequent, as can be seen from newspaper reports of the times. And riding and driving accidents figure in Matilda's novels as often as car accidents might in similar fiction today. There are a number of accidents caused by the rider or driver being drunk.

Katie Linwood's brother Stephen fell off his horse after a bout of drinking, broke both his legs and was soon dead, possibly from spinal injury (*Vermont Vale*). Although there was no accident Milly Ashwin and her brother and sister had a terrifying drive home after their visit to meet the family of Mabel Gordon whom John was soon to marry. They had all been plied with wine and Ellie's fiancé Percy drove not 'in his usual cool, handsome style, but in a wild random manner'. His 'boisterous laughter . . . rang out repeatedly on the night air' (*John's Wife*). The Hall brothers and their families arrived in Australia already sad with the story of their drunken brother and uncle Daniel who had lost control of his cart while driving under the influence of alcohol, had made 'violent contact' with a stationary waggon and tipped his passengers into a ditch. Dan was uninjured but his wife was killed, crushed beneath the cart (*Hall's Vineyard*). In the same novel a neighbour who was driving his waggon home and whose judgement had been impaired by Hall's 'strong colonial wine' let slip the reins which became entangled in the legs of one of the shaft-horses. The struggles of this horse alarmed the others and in panic they swung the waggon into a stump. The driver was thrown out and killed.

Herbert Gordon (*John's Wife*) called on Milly Ashwin in such a state of inebriation that she dared not open the door to him. Terrified that he would not reach his home safely she sent her maid with a note to her brother's office—a slow business as she had to walk. John sent someone riding after Herbert but he was too late. The man arrived in time to see him thrown—'pitched on his head as he fell'. Milly reflected in her journal: 'Poor Herbert! how horrible it seems. And this is but one out of hundreds of instances, almost of daily occurrence in this colony'. The problem of drinking and driving seems to be a longstanding one.

But not all those who are hurt are drunken drivers. Some of the most exemplary characters come to grief. Sober Kenneth Gordon riding rapidly to a chapel gathering on a thickly-shadowed track was 'pitched violently forward' off his horse when it stumbled into a newly-made excavation. Luckily two men riding behind him in a gig saw the accident, lifted him up and carried him to the nearest hotel. As he was destined to marry the heroine Beatrice, he soon recovered (*Beatrice Melton's Discipline*).

One of Matilda's last Christmas stories, written in 1884 especially for *The Chronicle*, gives a particularly interesting account of the prelude to and aftermath of an accident which has striking parallels with similar situations today. John collected orders and delivered goods for an Adelaide retail firm. He courted and married Annie, a parlour maid he had encountered when collect-ing orders at Rose Villa. (She was so ladylike that to begin with he had feared that she was a nursery governess which might have put her out of his reach.) The two opened a drapery in a country town and prospered. They were invited to take dinner on Christmas day at the Mastermans, 'large farmers about ten miles from our store'. They owned a vehicle in which John delivered goods, an 'old heavy cart—heavy from its clumsy construction, as well as from the wood it was made of, added to the heaviness of its springs and some most unnecessary iron bolts and appliances'. They had intended to buy a 'lighter and more modern equipage' but they had a baby and not much money and so decided to make do for one more year. 'We would just give the old thing a coat of paint to freshen it up and make it a wee more respectable.' They got the blacksmith to do the job and congratulated themselves on their economy. On Christmas day they set out with their baby and their maid Susie and considerable luggage to drive to the Mastermans. A steep hill badly rutted by recent rain worried John and he asked his passengers to alight until he was safely at the bottom. To his amusement Susie clung to the lunch-basket with its bottle of fresh milk. The track was covered with long grass and shrubs and was difficult to follow.

> We had come so far, however, very fairly, without any danger, and were half down the hill when suddenly the brake snapped. The whole weight of the vehicle came upon the horse's back, and no longer able to bear up against it he began a headlong course down the rest of the descent which I had no power to restrain. I had no time either to spring from the cart. I could do nothing absolutely but hold on and pray. It was but for a moment, a moment in which certain death appeared before my eyes. It seems to me I had only time to exclaim 'God help me and my poor wife', when we reached the bottom of the hill, and with a shock and a crash the old lumbering machine of a cart turned over and atop of me.
>
> 'How Annie Saved Me'

John was pinned beneath the cart, held prisoner by its weight with only his legs protruding, one of them broken. Annie and Susie hurried up and Susie was sent for help. (She lost her way and was rescued late that night.) Annie's resourcefulness was shown immediately when she sprayed soda-water on the ground (soda-water and lemonade were in the lunch-basket as gifts for the Mastermans) and scraped a hole big enough for John to slide his clasp knife under the side of the cart. This enabled her to break away part of a panel and get the bottle of milk in for John to drink from and to give him some light and air.

With the aid of knife spoon and soda-water she then excavated on either side of her prostrate husband depressions deep enough to allow her to push pieces of the broken shafts underneath the cart and so raise some of the weight from his legs. At length after much panting and struggling she was able to use a heavy flat stone as a further lever until the weight was entirely removed. They were both aware that unless the pressure was removed, morbidity would set in and he would lose his leg and probably his life. Annie then managed to cut away stocking and shoe from the broken swollen leg. Four hours later help arrived, the Mastermans having been alerted by the horse which had arrived at their gates with its broken harness.

While John spent many weeks immobilised at the Mastermans Annie ran the store. The old cart was then replaced with a 'handsome, commodious, light-springed trap'. Matilda did not point the moral. It was left to the readers to remember John's earlier statement that they had been 'penny wise and pound foolish'. They had had the old cart painted for appearances but had not had its brakes repaired. And once again one of Matilda's little ladylike wives has proved level-headed, tough and resourceful.

At the other end of the social scale were the vehicles of the wealthy. Mrs Norton, wife of the local member of Parliament, held little intercourse with the district community.

> She occasionally drove through the middle of the busy township in her stylish phaeton, honouring the doctor's wife and the lawyer's sister with a visit or an invitation, giving little of her custom to the tradespeople, and bestowing very condescending nods upon those who considered themselves both by birth and education her equal and her husband's superior.
>
> *The Master of Ralston*, p. 21

A phaeton was a light four-wheeled carriage, a prestigious vehicle. The Nortons may have owned more than one. At any rate the phaeton in which Alton later picked up the Valma girls seated at least five, not including a groom. A reviewer of the novel had pointed out that 'for the bloated "Hon. Percy Norton" ... we can all put that member of the Legislative Council whom we especially despise'. No doubt women readers had no difficulty in seeing in Mrs Norton some local dignitary at whose hands they had suffered and for whom they had little respect.

Blanche Norton too drove a 'low phaeton', an 'elegant equipage' with 'silver tracery' and 'pretty cream-coloured ponies' in which she might often be seen 'queening it' as in a 'triumphal car'. One of the difficulties in reading this fiction is to know whether or not a young girl like Blanche would herself be driving the phaeton, since the writer expected a degree of knowledge in her readers that we now do not have. It is clear that Blanche did drive, although her mother stipulated that she must always be accompanied by a groom, 'who sat with folded arms behind'. Blanche drove rapidly and with style, using a whip, 'a mere plaything', for 'the mere dash of the thing'.

Nelly Cameron in the same novel was used to driving herself and refused the accompaniment of a groom when she borrowed Bennett's buggy to drive to Amber Vale. Aunt Dunstan in *Golden Gifts* drove herself, although Thurza was not allowed to drive because she was by temperament too mercurial and untrustworthy. Men who we are told were out driving were probably— but not certainly—holding the reins themselves.

Also through the Nortons we get a different glimpse of a past world of transport; I found it surprisingly moving.

> 'Draw a little on one side, Nelly!' exclaimed her aunt suddenly. 'There are wheels coming down this road, from Amber Park, I suppose—very rapidly, too!'
> Nelly retreated to the side of the road, leaving space for the vehicle which was rapidly approaching. A moment after, a hooded buggy dashed by, in which Mrs Ralston caught a glimpse of two ladies, Mrs. and Miss Norton—she recognized them in spite of their heavy veils. After them presently came Alton Norton and his married brother, riding with a speed that indicated urgent necessity, and bid fair soon to distance the buggy. They were all out of sight in a moment, and Nelly and her aunt looked gravely after them, as they, too, drove quietly forward.
> 'Something is the matter at the Park,' said Mrs. Ralston seriously. 'People do not drive like that for nothing.'
> *The Master of Ralston*, p. 251

What had happened was the sudden illness of the Hon. Percy who had been 'attacked by a fit of apoplexy' and was not expected to live. Swiftly moving buggy and horses would certainly make a greater impact on passersby than today's motor vehicles.

What I have hoped to convey by this glimpse of methods of transport in the mid-nineteenth century is what a different world it was from our own and yet how similar in many respects. It gives a picture of a society in which women—providing they or their fathers or husbands had at least some money—had a surprising amount of freedom to move around. Even young girls could be independent and have a great deal of fun either driving or riding.

Of course their activities were curbed by the weather in a way that similar activities would not be today. Although many buggies and phaetons had adjustable hoods these would have been little protection against the heavy rains or the fierce hot north winds about which Matilda often wrote. Most of Matilda's hardworking young women did not have time for driving or access to buggies, although like the Valma girls they might sometimes be taken for drives by their friends. But many of them had horses or access to horses and carts, and even if they merely walked or rode or drove no further than the chapel they could lead free and fulfilling lives.

CHAPTER 14

Gentle Readers

I have been writing in this section not of Matilda Evans, about whom I have learnt from letters, from newspaper articles, from rate assessments, from the Board of Education minutes and other such factual records, but of another Matilda who must rightly be termed the 'implied author', a shadowy figure who cannot be known, but whose character and interests—whose very existence—I have deduced from my reading of her books. When so little is known of the real woman there is no alternative, but the distinction needs to be made.

And the readers I have often referred to were not real readers but 'implied readers', counterparts of the implied author, the unknown readers for whom the stories with all their assumptions about what is important and what is interesting have been shaped. Such a concept is important. Matilda Evans was writing for a particular public. Real readers today must adapt themselves to the moral, religious and cultural norms of her narratives and move at least some way in the direction of becoming the kind of readers she conjured up in her writings before they can begin to appreciate her and her world.

A further distinction needs to be made. The voice we hear narrating the novels is not the voice of the real Matilda Evans, nor of Evans as implied author. Maud Jeanne Franc is the narrator of these novels, a mature and confident narrating personality. Even when Matilda Congreve was herself quite young, Maud Jeanne Franc spoke with a firm and bold assurance. Matilda was by all accounts a quiet retiring person, but Franc is not Matilda. Franc projects a strong, confiding, expansive, even matronly, personality, one who believes herself in command of the truth and is ready to lay down the law.

Matilda was writing at a time when direct address from narrator to narratee—that is direct address from the 'voice' telling the story to a person or persons imagined to be reading the book—was an accepted method of establishing a relationship between real author and real reader. It has been out of fashion for some time now, but many of the great Victorian novelists were skilled practitioners of the method, and Matilda uses the technique naturally and comfortably.

Maud Jeanne Franc constantly attempts to draw her readers into her stories by addressing them directly or by speaking about them. 'Our readers', 'our young lady readers', 'our fair readers' and even 'my masculine readers' are some of those to whom she offers comment and advice. She exhorts 'young wives' to consider their husbands' needs, she forestalls guesses about possible lovers in a story by acknowledging a likely outcome—'yes, fair suspicious reader'—she speaks of her characters as 'our friends'. She asks direct questions: 'Have you, gentle reader, ever sat thus beside the sick, watching, fearfully watching, for the last breath to be drawn?' In this way Franc creates the persona of a solid reliable authoritative friend and mentor and suggests what sort of readers she expects to enjoy her stories.

The characteristics of the implied author are reconstructed from the novels taken as wholes, and the characteristics of Maud Jeanne Franc from the tones of the narrator. But what of her readers? Can we get beyond the narratee and the implied reader to those real readers of the past? Is it possible to discover, in 1994, who read these books and what they were like?

One young man has left a record. He was 'Cit', a journalist who wrote the 'Town Tattle' column for the Gawler paper *The Bunyip*. In September 1904 he wrote in an obituary for his friend, Matilda's younger son Willie Evans, that 'I was influenced in London to make Adelaide my home through reading one of his mother's novels'. The assumption has sometimes been made that the novels of Maud Jeanne Franc are negligible because they were written for children and read by girls. That 'Cit' was moved to come to Adelaide suggests that they reached a wider audience.

What that wider audience was like so many years ago is now difficult to discover, but I believe it is possible to make some deductions about it. A recent book by Martyn Lyons and Lucy Taksa, *Australian Readers Remember*, takes the first 'exploratory steps' towards the writing of 'the history of the Australian reader'. Lyons and Taksa interviewed a number of elderly residents of New South Wales and from their memories built up a picture of what was read and how it was responded to at the beginning of this century.

Though the name of Maud Jeanne Franc is not mentioned in this book the world of reading conjured up has much in common with world of reading to be found in Franc's novels, and many of Lyons's and Taksa's comments are relevant to an understanding of what Franc's readers might have been like. They found for instance that 'buying a book is only one of many ways of obtaining something to read'. There are 'informal distribution networks through which reading matter circulates—through families, work-mates, library borrowers or trade union members'. They say also that 'Book historians should not, therefore, measure a book's pop-ularity solely by its circulation figures'. I have no circulation fig-ures for Franc's novels, but the fact that there are well over 400 copies preserved in Australian collections alone, and that copies over 100 years old can still be found in bookshops, suggests that her novels were treasured and preserved by those who owned them—and without doubt they were read by many more people than their original owners. I have recorded over 150 inscriptions as I have sought out copies of Franc's books and from these many deductions can be made. This information will I believe add a little more to the history of books and reading in Australia.

Many copies have not only signatures, but dates and places, and in some cases booksellers' stickers, so that it is possible to know now that copies were bought and sold in Adelaide, Sydney, Brisbane, Melbourne and Hobart, and that copies travelled from these outlets all over Australia. In South Australia copies bear the place names of Angaston, Ashton, Coromandel Valley, Cowell, Direk, Kapunda, Melrose, Mount Gambier, Murray Town,

Second Valley, Terowie, Truro, Two Wells, Woodchester and Yeelanna, as well as of many of the inner suburbs of Adelaide. In Victoria copies are recorded from Ascot Vale, Elsternwick, Hamilton, Horsham, Melbourne, and Warrnambool; in New South Wales from Bexley, Bomaderry, Croydon, Darlinghurst, Dulwich Hill, Hunters Hill, Newtown and Tabbita; in Queensland from Brisbane and Pullenvale, and in Tasmania from Hobart —one so early as to be from Hobart Town—and Sidmouth. There are also copies with place names I have not been able to find and other place names, like Brighton and Sydenham, which are found in more than one state.

A copy can be shown to have moved from Tabbita in central New South Wales to Direk, a district just north of Adelaide. Another spent over one hundred years in an area in the north of South Australia. In 1888 a copy of *Silken Cords* became part of the collection of the Wesleyan Sunday school at Melrose. Later it joined the library of the Bible Christian Sunday school at Murray Town, about 13 kilometres south. It was found in 1993 in an antique shop in Orroroo some 60 kilometres north-east of Melrose. A copy of *Vermont Vale* was recently found in Nuriootpa, a town close to the area where the story is set.

Many copies have more than one signature, suggesting that copies were handed down in families and passed on to friends, as well as given away or sold. A copy of *Marian* in the Emu binding has two inscriptions: 'To Laura from Mother, August 6th 1911', and 'To Dear Merle from Grandpop, December 13th 1963'. It seems reasonable to deduce—since the copy is now in the Library and Information Service of W.A.—that Merle did not treasure it as her forebear Laura had done.

Sometimes the same name appears on a number of titles, suggesting that the pleasure of reading one book had led to the acquisition of others: Emily Hansom was given a copy of *Silken Cords* which is inscribed 'To Emily Hansom with love and best wishes for her future happiness from R. Edwards' but she later wrote her name in copies of *No Longer A Child*, *Little Mercy* and *Into The Light*. These have survived—there may have been others.

M.M. Barlow wrote her name in several copies but one at least was given to her on 9 October 1884 'in remembrance of October 9 1882'. Some of Barlow's copies were acquired by E.C. Fuller who sometimes wrote the signature and sometimes stamped it. Some of these copies later came into the collection of Harold L. Sheard and bear his bookplate. I suspect that Harold Sheard was a book collector, but I do not think E.C. Fuller was. A copy with the signature M. Fuller also has the Sheard bookplate. It seems likely that members of the Fuller family bought some copies new and acquired some secondhand. These later formed part of the Sheard collection.

Copies in other collections also have personal associations. There are over 50 copies of Franc's novels in the Mitchell library—but two copies, an 1866 *Vermont Vale* and an 1881 *Emily's Choice* bear the signature of David Scott Mitchell himself. Thomas Gill, compiler of the 1886 *Bibliography of South Australia*, was also a collector and his copies of Franc's novels, many of them from the famous York Gate Library, are now in the library of the South Australian branch of the Royal Geographical Society. The first edition of *Little Mercy* however was the personal copy of his wife Louisa and bears her signature.

Some of the inscriptions reflect the joy and excitement associated with the occasion of giving and suggest that for some readers Franc's books were believed to be in themselves meaningful gifts. A first edition of *Two Sides* carries the words 'To our own Dear Clare wishing her many happy returns of the day and Every success during her life from her loving companions in Training, Emma, Maggie, Mary and A[...] Melbourne'. A first edition of *Into the Light* has the inscription 'To Nellie Brookes From her affectionate Friend Fannie Isaacs as a token of love and esteem towards her. Xmas 1890'. Another first edition of *Into the Light* bears the signature of Alice J. Latham, of Angaston, with the words 'A Gift from Dear Mrs Ayliffe In Remembrance of my dear Clare's Wedding Day'. Alice Latham also owned a copy of *Marian* with the date 1880 inscribed.

Something can often be deduced of the age and sex of the owners of inscribed copies. Certainly these books were not all given to children. There are many copies which bear inscriptions showing that they had been given to married women. 'To Mrs R. Hopkins with love from L. Willcocks' and 'Mrs Large. A birthday present from Lizzie' are examples.

The Mortlock Library's copy of *Silken Cords* which bears my grandmother's signature (and which I very much regret was not handed on to me!) could not have been acquired by her before she reached the age of thirty-five or forty. She was born in 1862 and the Leaf binding of her copy of *Silken Cords* was a turn-of-the-century binding and may even have been as late as 1905.

There are copies from mothers to daughters and from daughters to mothers, from brothers to sisters ('To Emily Burford. A Christmas present from her brother Robert'), from grandparents ('To Dear Henry wishing him many happy returns of the day from Granma. 72 Walter St. Ascot Vale. May 1913') and from aunts ('Presented to John G Hallam by his affectionate Aunt 6/5/91'). Some copies were twenty-first birthday presents. Only two copies make it clear that the recipients were children: one copy of *Minnie's Mission* is inscribed 'To Dear Flo on her 14th Birthday from Ern and Fan April 19, 1894' and another 'Agnes Golding from her brother David on her 12th birthday'.

A surprising number carry male names or bookplates. Maybe some of these were book collectors, but clearly not all were. Charles Jackson was presented with a copy of *Vermont Vale* on 24 December 1866, and Allan Rogers received *John's Wife* as a school prize as late as 1918.

In England Franc's publishers were listing her works in their catalogues as 'suitable for school prizes and presents' by 1875. In Australia her books were given as school and Sunday school prizes from as early as 1869. There are school stickers or inscriptions from Pullenvale School, Warrnambool Grammar School, Tonsley House, Sydenham Ladies' College, Mount Mary School, Waratah Public School and the Church of England Day Schools.

The books were even more popular as Sunday school prizes or as books in Sunday school libraries. Methodist, Wesleyan, Salvation Army, Church of Christ, Congregational, Bible Christian and Anglican churches all participated. The writer of the obituary of 'Maud Jean Franc' published in *The Christian Colonist*, who declared 'No Sunday-school library should be considered furnished which does not contain a complete set of her writings', had himself 'when a lad' read 'with considerable interest a local story entitled "Marian"' and had gone on to read other books by the same writer.

The Chronicle reported on 12 July 12 1884 that on the previous Sunday children's services had been held at the Smithfield Presbyterian Church. Sixty children received a book prize and in addition five prizes were given to the Sunday school teachers for essays written in response to a challenge by Mr H.J. Congreve who was their preacher. These extra prizes for the teachers were 'five volumes of works written by Maud Jean Franc, the sister of Mr. Congreve'. And prizes were also given by other groups. The New South Wales Woman's Society for the Prevention of Cruelty to Animals gave a copy of *Vermont Vale* to the winner of an essay competition on the subject of bees.

Not only Sunday School libraries stocked these books. Public Libraries and Institute Libraries also held copies, many having been rebound for library use. Stickers give some of the information which follows; other details I have gathered from catalogues of the institutions themselves. Unfortunately few such lists have survived. The Public Library of South Australia, the Adelaide Circulating Library and the libraries of the Institutes at Kapunda, Port Adelaide, Saddleworth, Semaphore and Truro in South Australia and Horsham in Victoria all held copies. Brighton Public Library [Victoria?] accessioned a copy of *Vermont Vale* as late as December 1933. T.L. Hood's Select Circulating Library at 60 Liverpool Street Hobart, which lent books from one guinea per annum, also stocked Maud Jeanne Franc. A first edition of *Into the Light* was in a Y.M.C.A. Library. The Presbyterian Church of Victoria ran a Chaplaincy Committee Library for the Melbourne Hospital. Copies of novels by Franc from this Library, originally bought much earlier, were presented to the Public Library of Victoria in 1925.

Clearly Franc's novels were read widely in Australia. Although I have not found any copies with information which links them to Western Australia the presence of a number of copies in the

Library and Information Service of W.A. suggests that they were read there too.

And it was not only in Australia that these books made an impact. A reviewer of *Into The Light* (very likely her brother Henry) writing in *The Bunyip* on 19 May 1885 pointed out the scope of her readership. 'Her works, which at first had but a local demand, are now to be found not only in the neighbouring colonies, but in America and England.' A brother may be partial, but there is supp rting evidence for this claim.

The seven copies listed in the Library of Congress *National Union Catalog—Pre 1956 Imprints*, which range from the first novel, *Marian*, to one of the last, *'Two Sides to Every Question'*, prove that her work was known in the United States. The reader who dated her copy of *Emily's Choice* 'April 1925' and wrote in it 'I bought this copy in Bath in England' had obviously found in it a bookshop. It is a copy in the Hockey binding and according to the *English Catalogue of Books* was not due for release until May of 1925. It was therefore not a copy which had been collecting dust on the shelves, but a bright new copy and in a provincial town at that.

If I had had the time and the means I would have enjoyed tracking Franc's books in the United Kingdom as I have in Australia —I am sure I would have found some. As it is I must rely on other information. J. S. Bratton's *The Impact of Victorian Children's Fiction* provides evidence that Franc's works were among the prize and library titles of the London School Board which bought books for the Board Schools from the early 1870s. By the mid 1890s as tastes changed religious novels like Franc's lost favour. Bratton quotes the Rev. A.W. Jephson as writing of her novels 'I do not like these books: the tone is bad, the teaching of the narrowest, and the style inferior' (p. 195). It is true that Franc was not a stylist and that the teaching is narrow, but it is likely that Jephson was influenced, as so many male critics were at the time, by an inability to see the value of books which dealt with domestic issues. At any rate it seems very likely that Franc's books were on prize and library lists in England just as they were in Australia.

I own a copy of *Golden Gifts*, dated 23 January 1914, which bears a prize sticker from the Hertford Corps of the Salvation Army. From 1919 to 1938 the Salvation Army promoted a scheme for British people to migrate to Australia. It seems likely that this copy accompanied its migrant owner to Australia. Indeed, the pioneering nature of the story of *Golden Gifts* and the promising picture of Australian life it presents may well have contributed to the willingness of the family to migrate.

And 'Cit', too, who was prompted to come to Adelaide by reading one of Franc's novels obviously found his copy—sometime in the 1870s—in the United Kingdom. An obituary published in *The Publishers' Circular* on 6 December 1886 spoke of Matilda Evans as 'this talented colonial writer' and added 'Mrs Evans' books are well-known in this country, although the author is more familiar to British readers by her pen-name Maude Jeanne Franc'.

There is another aspect of these books which throws light on their readers. Lyons and Taksa in *Australian Readers Remember* found that much of the reading at the beginning of this century was related to religion. Writing of the 'world of reading we have lost' they noted the importance in earlier years of 'the presence of the family Bible, the practice of group reading in a religious context, and the respect which books inspired as physical objects' (p. 29). This is the 'world of reading' to be found in Franc's novels. Her 'good' characters are defined by the presence of the family Bible and the use to which it is put.

> But the masterpiece of all was to come; for when the neat-handed maiden, in her short, dark print dress and white apron, had carried away the last of the supper dishes, she came back into the room, and, placing the large green baize book before her master, retreated modestly to a chair at the side.
>
> James Foster opened the great book before him, slowly, reverently. He made no excuses, asked no forbearance on our part. It was one of the customs of the house—as much so as the breakfast on the table in the morning, as the supper spread for our repast at night. He had not a suspicion that an excuse was needed, and I respected him for it.
>
> I shall never forget that reading, or the way the rich old Bible words rolled out, as though every word was loved and believed in. I do not know whether I had ever noticed that

twenty-seventh Psalm before; certainly I had never thought it
so full of beauty, so expressive of what I needed.

Into The Light, p. 41

Readings from the family Bible, personal Bible readings, family
prayers, reading hymns together: these form an important part of
a number of Franc's books, particularly of the early ones and of
Into The Light. Present-day students of past reading habits can
discover something about them by reading Franc's novels.

Lyons and Taksa made no mention of hymns in their study of
reading habits. Possibly none of their subjects remembered hymn
reading as part of family activities, though it seems unlikely since I
have memories myself of the reading and sharing of favourite
hymns on Sunday afternoons in the late 1920s. But certainly
Franc's characters read and quoted hymns frequently, knowing
many by heart, and the narrator of *Marian*, *Vermont Vale* and
Emily's Choice, particularly, used them constantly in her religious
teaching. Hymn reading as well as hymn singing was a part of
this world.

George Thomas Congreve, Matilda's brother, compiled a
hymn book—*Gems of Song for the Sunday School*—to which he
contributed a number of hymns himself. I have seen a copy of
this little book. It is indeed very small—7 × 11 cm and less then a
centimetre thick. It would rest easily in a child's hand, would slip
into a pocket, under a pillow or into a handbag. It seems very
likely that it was used by Matilda in her schools.

Many of Franc's readers would not have been surprised to find
Bible readings and hymns an integral part of her stories, and they
would surely have agreed with her when she called hymn writers
poets or 'sacred' poets. Many hymn writers are mentioned by
name, especially Dr Watts, Augustus Toplady—author of 'Rock of
Ages'—the 'Christian poet Montgomery', and among women the
'Honourable Mrs Norton', Frances Havergal and 'sweet Mary
Howitt'.

Matilda's own reading is of course being shown here, reading
which it is reasonable to assume she shared with many of those
who read her books. More information about what was read at
least by educated colonists can also be discovered when attention

is paid to the many writers Matilda quotes or refers to.

Most well-known poets from Chaucer and Spenser to her own times are quoted, sometimes as epigraphs to chapters. Keats, Tennyson and Longfellow appear, as well as lesser lights like Bryant, Bernard Barton, Thomas Haynes Bayley, Martin Tupper and R.H. Dana. Wordsworth is extensively quoted and almost all her novels have references to Shakespeare. Less likely references are to Ben Jonson, *Hudibras*, 'Junius' and *Don Quixote*. There are far too many writers for me to list or quote them all. When we remember that Matilda was only twenty-four when she arrived in Adelaide it is clear that much of this reading must have been done in South Australia. Knowing the circumstances of her life I am impressed by the range of her reading.

This survey of readers and reading would not be complete without a reference to another source of information about the way readers found out about Franc's books. Advertisements appeared in Adelaide papers over a period of thirty years, from the initial advertisements for the parts of *Marian* in May 1859 to the advertisements for the uniform posthumous edition in July 1888.

While books by other writers usually received single lines in booksellers' lists the novels of Maud Jeanne Franc as they appeared were given separate bold advertisements between one and two centimetres in height. Booksellers Platts, Rigby, Wigg, Howell and Robertson all at some time advertised Franc's work. In 1869 for instance *The Register* ran Rigby, Wigg and Howell advertisements for *Minnie's Mission* from 1 October until 21 December.

In such cases the advertisements were frequently in the same column, sometimes indeed absolutely underneath one another, enabling potential buyers to make interesting comparisons. In this particular case W.C. Rigby, 53 Hindley-Street, offered *Minnie's Mission* at '4s. 6d.; per post 6s.', while J. Howell, 4 Rundle-Street, gave the price as '4s.; by post 5s. 2d.' Rigby's price was excessive. Books printed in England were at that time normally sold in Australia at the same price as they were sold in England. The price of *Minnie's Mission* should have been 4s.

Wigg's advertisement merely stated 'New Tale by the

Authoress of "Marian", "Minnie's Mission" just received by E.S. Wigg'. E.S. Wigg was of course one of the leading members of the Baptist Church in South Australia and Wigg Booksellers were Franc's most faithful advertisers, but most local papers carried advertisements at one time or another.

Often accompanying advertisements for particular titles were reminders that all the works of the author were in stock. In the 1880s *The Chronicle* in its notices for the Christmas supplements advertised that stories had been specially written for the issues by Maud Jeanne Franc.

It was not only reviews then which kept Franc's name before the South Australian public. Advertisements were important too, but probably equally important were the affection felt by readers for the books they already owned and their willingness to recommend and to lend them.

Conclusion

I cannot make great claims for Matilda Evans as a novelist, although I believe her work is not negligible and should be better known, at least in her own state. As a public figure—as a novelist, as a teacher and as a church worker—she made her mark in the South Australia of her time and we should honour her among our pioneers.

Her novels are outside the mainstream of Australian fiction. They fit none of the stereotypes, especially not that of the battler from the bush pitted against the hostilities of nature. *Marian*, actually described in the subtitle as 'A Tale of Australian Bush Life', does not present life in the bush as a struggle against a hostile environment. Nature is presented not as harsh and unrelenting but as benign and bountiful. It is the behaviour of people, not nature, which causes problems for the farmers and country dwellers in these novels. There are hot winds and droughts and frosts, rains and floods but they are minor obstacles which are taken in their stride by the characters. Even the terrible bushfires which destroy the properties of the Wallace family in *Golden Gifts* and the Russel family in 'Underneath: A Christmas Day's Revelations' (*The Chronicle*, 19 December 1885) are presented as natural disasters rather than as manifestations of hostile nature.

Franc was a writer of limited ability. Her style is pedestrian, her insights prosaic, but she faithfully portrayed the world she knew. She reflected what she saw, emphasised what she believed to be important, and attempted to influence the shape of events to come. She knew that not all the members of the society in which she lived were as fervent in their religious beliefs as she was and that not all shared her views on temperance. She endeavoured in her novels to help create a world—a South Australian world—in which people might learn to accept the values she believed in.

It is frequently stated that colonial women writers wrote for the English market, but I believe that that is not true of Matilda Evans. Nine of her fourteen novels—and all of the early ones—were published in Australia before they were published in England. And although she occasionally in her later novels addressed 'my English readers' it was with her adult Australian readers, their behaviour, their beliefs and the world they lived in, with which she was concerned. The picture she gave of South Australian society reflected what she approved as well as what she disapproved, and in this way helped to shape a South Australian middle class which was freer and more egalitarian than its English counterpart.

And her novels provided role models for young South Australian men and women—especially for women. Her woman characters, however fragile they seem, are frequently tougher and more independent than the men. The women and girls who read her stories might not have been conscious of this, but might still have been strengthened in conducting their own lives by observing the steadfastness of characters like Marian and Emily.

It is impossible to gauge the extent of her influence in her own time. Knowing the effect of my own reading upon me in the days before the ubiquity of radio, film and television I suspect that it was considerable. I did not read Maud Jeanne Franc, but I read her American counterpart Elizabeth Wetherell, and her books made an unforgettable impact upon me. The extent of the popularity of Franc's novels—which is further substantiated in the Bibliography of her work which follows—suggests that her influence was considerable.

Because of their lack of attention to the concerns which have dominated Australian writing, because of their concentration on religious and domestic themes, and their preoccupation with temperance issues, because of their mildness and their narrowness, these novels have in the past not recommended themselves to literary historians. The growth of women's studies in present times perhaps opens the way for a new interest in both the work of Maud Jeanne Franc and the achievements of Matilda Evans.

*Daisy binding for the first posthumous uniform edition of
Maud Jeanne Franc's novels in 1888.*

Frontispiece for Vermont Vale *(1866) by George French Angas.*
(Mortlock Collection)

Frontispiece for Emily's Choice *(1867) by George French Angas.*

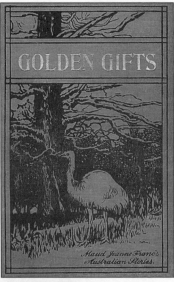

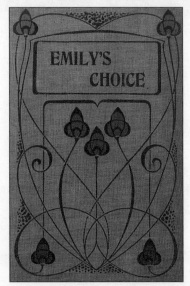

Early twentieth century bindings
Single daisy binding 1900–1905   Emu binding 1911–1918
Poppy binding 1914–1919

PART THREE

An Annotated Bibliography
of the Works of
MAUD JEANNE FRANC

together with a checklist of the writings of
HENRY JOHN CONGREVE

Appealing to 1920s schoolgirls. A cover and two dustjackets.
(Mortlock Collection)

Publishing History

Tracing the publishing history of the novels of Maud Jeanne Franc has produced a fascinating picture of how a major nineteenth-century publishing company, Sampson Low, dealt with the work of a very minor colonial novelist whose novels, published in England between 1860 and 1885, were popular enough to have a steady, though obviously small, sale.

The novels were kept in print until well into this century, but the issues were probably not large. Sheets and settings of type were stored for many years; in some cases the original settings of type were used for fifty years or more. Sheets were bound as required with little regard for the anomalies this often caused. Usually new title pages were added for new impressions, but sometimes copies have title-page dates that precede by a number of years the first use of the binding in which they appear. Sometimes a copy bears an advertisement announcing that it is one of a uniform series with a price which belongs to a much more expensive binding than the one in which it appears. Dates—often very different from those on title pages—on bound-in catalogues, particularly for issues in the Rose binding, suggest that copies were bound year by year as the need arose.

As an investigator I soon learned to distrust title pages and advertisements, but also to respect both the publisher, who was unwilling to waste any sheets in his possession, and the author, whose moral and improving colonial tales continued to command sufficient interest to make it worth the publisher's while to reissue them constantly.

Maud Jeanne Franc's first novel, *Marian, or The Light of Someone's Home*, was first published in 1859 in South Australia by Alfred Waddy of Mount Barker. The four parts were issued monthly from June to September. During this time, perhaps with the aid of George Thomas Congreve, the author's half-brother who lived in Surrey, an English publisher was found, Binns & Goodwin of Bath, a publisher specialising in religious works, whose name appeared on the title page at the back of the last of the four parts of *Marian* published at Mount Barker. Waddy of Mount Barker and Darton & Co. of London were co-publishers with Binns & Goodwin of the first English edition in 1860, and of the second in 1861. In 1862 Darton & Co. became Darton & Hodge, and when the third edition appeared towards the end of 1865, the names of Binns & Goodwin and Waddy had been relegated to small type at the bottom of the title page beneath Darton & Hodge. Early in 1866 Hodge and Darton went separate ways somewhat acrimoniously, and Sampson Low, who published *Vermont Vale* in April 1866 became Franc's sole publisher.

The third edition of *Marian*, published by Sampson Low, was reissued in 1867 in a new binding, with reset type. From then on Sampson Low, with various partners, published all Franc's work in England until publication ceased in the late nineteen-twenties. Eight of Franc's novels were published serially in newspapers or magazines in Australia before being published in England, and two, *Golden Gifts* and *Silken Cords*, were published in South Australia in book form.

Matilda Jane Congreve, later Evans, adopted the pseudonym Maud Jean Franc in 1859. By 1862 she was sometimes using the form Maud Jeanne Franc, which has become the preferred option for cataloguers, but the words Maud Jean Franc were still appearing on title pages in the 1920s. The variations Maude Jean Franc and Maude Jeanne Franc are frequently found and sometimes the spelling Jeane. An oddity of the publication of her work is that sometimes two different versions occur on the cover and spine of a single title, and frequently the spelling on the cover is not the same as that on the title page.

In the following pages I describe a first edition of each book and, when that is Australian, a first English edition also, state where the described copy is to be found—in most cases of course there are identical copies in other collections—and add comments on subsequent editions and reissues. This builds up a picture of a writer whose work was, in a small way and with a particular public, consistently popular over a period of seventy years. I have had access only to copies available in Australia where national pride has assisted in their preservation, but it is inconceivable that Sampson Low kept the novels in print purely to satisfy a colonial market.

They were read extensively in the United Kingdom and in the USA as well. The British Museum has them all, and the Library of Congress *National Union Catalog—pre 1956 Imprints* lists seven copies:

two in the New York Public Library—*Emily's Choice* (1875) and *Golden Gifts* (1869)—and five in the library of the University of North Carolina—*Marian* (1873), *Emily's Choice* (1875), *Golden Gifts* (1888), *Silken Cords* (n.d.) and *'Two Sides To Every Question'* (1883).

Although the words Second, Third, etc. Edition appear often on title pages, in many cases these were merely reissues with updated title pages. I have noted genuine new editions. Although many nineteenth-century re-issues were obviously bound up from sheets held in stock, there must also have been new impressions over the years. This is clear from the fact that although the type was apparently not reset for any of the copies issued after Franc's death in 1886, the quality of the paper used and the standard of printing deteriorated markedly between 1900 and the late 1920s.

Perhaps because Franc's novels were always popular with young people and because they were part of the school and Sunday school prize market over a period of sixty years, they were constantly re-issued in different bindings (i.e. publisher's casings), some of them very attractive. *Marian* today exists in over a dozen different bindings and even Franc's last novel, *The Master of Ralston*, can be found in at least six.

From 1888, when the first of the cheaper uniform editions was issued, many title pages bear no date. Information about bindings can help to assign approximate dates to these later issues. Other copies without dates can be assigned to particular years because Sampson Low changed partners so frequently. Changes in the firm of Gilbert and Rivington who were the principal printers used by Low for Franc's books between 1873 and 1905 also help to assign dates.

Publishers

Sampson Low, Son & Marston	1863-71
Sampson Low, Marston, Low & Searle	1871-75
Sampson Low, Marston, Searle & Rivington	1875-87
Sampson Low, Marston, Searle & Rivington Ltd.	1888-90
Sampson Low, Marston & Co. Ltd	1891-1930

Printers

Gilbert & Rivington, Ltd., St John's Square, London.	1873-1888
Gilbert & Rivington, Ltd., St John's House, Clerkenwell, London, E.C.	1888-1905

Binding Variants

I describe those bindings which appear to have been used for all four-teen titles and in addition those for the 1920s reprints of six titles. They are listed in chronological order.

Rose Binding: 11.5 × 17.7 cm. Deep maroon or purple cloth stamped in black on the front and back covers and in gold on the spine. The covers have ruled black borders and centred close to the spine is a black oblong from which a rose and leaves stand out in relief. The spine has a gold stylised floral decoration and gold bands from which the title, author's name—always MAUD JEANNE FRANC, whatever variation appears on the title page—and publisher's imprint—LON-DON SAMPSON LOW & Co.—stand out in relief. The pages have gilt edges. This binding was first used for the third edition of *Vermont Vale* in 1876, but between 1876 and 1886 all of Franc's novels appeared in it including six first editions.

There are some copies of other titles dated earlier—as early as 1869—but the dates on bound-in catalogues show that they did not appear until 1876 or after. Some copies of *Emily's Choice* are dated 1875, but copies in the original binding were still being issued in 1875 and those in the Rose binding usually have bound-in catalogues dated later. Copies in the Rose binding were sold for 5s. or 4s. Although this was the earliest and most expensive of the uniform editions the fact that over 100 copies can be found today in Australian collections suggests that they were widely distributed and very popular at the time.

Daisy Binding: 11.5 × 17.7 cm. Various coloured cloths, mainly shades of green, blue and grey, stamped in black and printed in white on the front cover and spine, with gold lettering of title and author—MAUD JEAN FRANC, whatever spelling appears on the title page—on the spine. There are five large white daisies enclosed in a circle on the front cover with the title in a slanted oblong near the top beneath another daisy. The name MAUD JEAN FRANC appears in a box at bottom right. The back cover is plain except for the publisher's device stamped in black in the centre.

This binding appeared first in 1888, two years after Franc's death, when all fourteen novels were issued in the first cheap edition at 2s. 6d. There are copies in this binding with title-page dates as late as 1891.

Silver Floral Binding: 11.5 × 17.7 cm. Finely ribbed cloths in various deep colours, mainly blue, green and maroon, stamped in silver—probably aluminium—on the front cover and spine in a rich design of sweetpea flowers and leaves. The title appears in silver in a plain box near the top of the front cover. The spine carries the title at the top, the author's name—MAUD JEAN FRANC—in a circle near the bottom, and the publisher's imprint—SAMPSON LOW MARSTON & Co.—below that.

While I have seen only twelve of Franc's novels in this binding an advertisement in each volume states that it was a uniform binding for all fourteen. The price was 2s. 6d. These appeared, not always with dates, between 1888 and 1895. Silver stamping was new at the time and it seems that interest in Franc's work was sufficient to justify this binding as well as the Daisy binding.

Leaf Binding: 11.4 × 18.3 cm. Light or dark green or blue cloth stamped in black on the front and in black and gold on the spine. Four long sprays of leaves, printed in varying shades of green, yellow and red, spread upwards on the front cover. There are four uncoloured bunches of berries. In the centre of the front cover a gold blocked rectangle allows the black letters of the title to stand out in relief. The words MAUD JEAN FRANC appear at bottom right in a scroll. A single spray of leaves runs up the spine. The title is stamped in gold at the top of the spine, in the centre a gold stamp allows the words MAUD JEAN FRANC to stand out in relief and the publisher's imprint—S. LOW. MARSTON & Co.— is stamped in gold at the base. On the back cover there is a small leaf spray at the top and a publisher's device with three leaves at the bottom.

All the novels were published in this binding between 1888 and 1905, although not all carry dates. It may be that some appeared even later. These sold at 2s. 6d. and at 2s. Copies which have 5s. or 4s. on advertisements on the verso of the title page were bound from sheets presumably prepared originally for the Rose binding. Novels by other writers who were published by Low, notably Louisa Alcott, also appeared in this binding.

Single Daisy Binding: 12.2 × 19 cm. Red cloth, blocked in gold and printed in white and green on the front cover and spine. The front cover has a green ruled border, the title in gold at the top, a single white daisy with two small buds printed at the centre and the words

MAUD JEANNE FRANC, or in some cases MAUD J. FRANC, printed in white at the bottom. (These are smaller: 11.5 × 17.9 cm.) The
spine has thin green printed bands, the title in gold in a green box at
the top, the words MAUD JEAN FRANC (Jean is spelt differently on
the cover!), or in some cases MAUD J. FRANC, and the publisher's
imprint—S.LOW. MARSTON & Co.— at the bottom. A smaller ver-
sion of the daisy motif appears three times. The back cover is blank.

I have found only seven titles in this binding, but advertisements
on the verso of title pages state that all titles were issued. These were
sold initially at 2s. 6d., later at 2s. and finally at 1s. when they were
reprinted on cheaper paper. Novels by other writers who were published by Low, notably Louisa Alcott, also appeared in this binding.

Gilbert & Rivington appear to have been the printers for all the
bindings described above, except where sheets left from earlier
editions were used.

Emu Binding: 12.3 × 18.8 cm Various coloured cloths, printed in
black and blocked in gold. On the front cover inside a double ruled
black border there is a design in black of a tall tree in a forest, with a
large emu below it. The title is blocked in gold in a box near the top
and the words 'Maud Jeanne Franc's Australian Stories' are printed in
black at bottom right. At the top of the spine the title, and the words
M.J. FRANC are blocked in gold. At the bottom the publisher's
imprint—SAMPSON LOW AND CO. LTD.—is also blocked in gold.
In between, printed in black, stands a kangaroo under two small trees.
The most usual binding has three gold triangles on the spine beneath
the title, but sometimes there is a gold line and sometimes there is no
gold decoration. Sometimes the kangaroo design is much smaller with
a single tree trunk instead of two.

There are no dated title pages (except when sheets left from earlier printings were used) but the many inscribed copies suggest that
books in this binding were available between 1911 and 1918. (I have
found 24 inscriptions with dates, all between March 1911 and Advent
1918.) Books in the Emu binding are not all the same size. Some
(11.5 × 17.9 cm.) appear to have been bound from small sheets printed by Gilbert & Rivington before 1905 and still in stock, but most
from larger newly-printed sheets.

The printers used later were usually Iredale-Brown & Sons or
Rea & Inchbould, though Kent & Matthews printed *Minnie's Mission*.
This edition, which sold for 1s., testifies to the popularity of Franc's

work early this century. I have located more than 60 copies in collections in Australia, far more than for any binding except the Rose binding.

Poppy Binding: 12.5 × 19.3 cm. Fawn or light brown cloth, stamped on the front cover in black and on the spine in black and gold, with stylised—art nouveau—poppy buds overprinted in red. The front cover has the title in a box near the top and seven buds on long thin black stems rising from the centre at the bottom, four of them curving towards the corners. On the spine the title and the words M.J. FRANC in gold are near the top with one bud above, and three on long stems below. The publisher's imprint—S. LOW. MARSTON & Co.—is printed in black at the bottom. The back cover is blank.

Advertisements on the verso of the title pages state that all fourteen titles were published in this binding at 1s, although I have found only seven. There are no dates for this binding, but five inscriptions, three for 1914, one for 1915 and one for 1917, give a good idea of when it was used. On the verso of the title page of the Mortlock Library's copy of *Minnie's Mission* are the words 'Printed by W. Mate & Sons (1919) Ltd'. Otherwise the printers are the same as for the Emu binding.

Hockey *and* ***Lacrosse Bindings:*** 12.2 × 19 cm. Red cloth stamped in black on the front cover and spine.
Hockey *variation:* the front cover has a double black border, with the title and MAUD JEAN FRANC in a box towards the top and a design of three schoolgirls below. One carries a hockey stick and another a tennis racquet. Running down the spine from the title and the words M. J. FRANC at the top to the publisher's imprint—SAMPSON LOW—at the bottom is a design resembling a totem pole. The back cover is blank.
Lacrosse *variation:* there is no black border or box on the front cover, and instead of the hockey and tennis girls are two girls carrying lacrosse sticks.

These books, each with a frontispiece by M.L.P. showing some of the characters in 1920s clothes, appeared between 1925 and 1930. There is usually another illustration by M.L.P. later in the text. (I have been unable to identify this illustrator.) Several of the brightly coloured dustjackets in which it seems likely that they were all issued have survived.

Only six titles, selling at 2s. 6d., were reprinted in this binding: *Vermont Vale*, *Emily's Choice*, and *Minnie's Mission*, appeared in 1925 and *Marian*, *Beatrice Melton's Discipline* and *The Master of Ralston* in the next couple of years.

At the same time *Marian* appeared as well in a **Plain Red Binding**, with the title stamped in black at the top of the front cover and MAUD JEAN FRANC at the bottom. There is no totem design on the spine. Otherwise the spine is similar to that on the Hockey and Lacrosse bindings. All these late printings were by Purnell and Sons, Paulton, Somerset, England. The fact that *Marian* was issued in all three of these bindings suggests that while most of Franc's books were now seen as being attractive to schoolgirls *Marian* could still be marketed for adults. All six books were obviously still popular in the 1920s. Over forty copies survive in Australian collections.

List of Publications

1859

MARIAN or The Light Of Someone's Home. A Tale of Australian Bush Life.
BY MAUD JEAN FRANC. Mount Barker: Alfred Waddy, Gilles
Street. Adelaide: William Hallows Hillier. Eighteen Pence. Part 1,
June 1859.
4 vols. 11 × 18.4 cm. Printer: Alfred Waddy.
Vol. I: pp. 1-72. Vol. 2: pp. 73-144. Vol.3: pp. 145-216. Vol. 4: pp.
217-262.

There are no title pages; title page information is given on the covers.
These parts were issued in pale blue, green, yellow, orange, and rose
paper covers, more than one colour being used for each part. The
covers are printed in black. On the front cover the word MARIAN is
in tall bold letters. The words on the front covers are surrounded by a
thin scalloped black border outside which there is a thinner stylised
decoration. Parts 2, 3 and 4 have the printer's name beneath the
decorated border. The back covers contain notices of two other
publications by Waddy and for the first three parts the publisher's
advertisement for the succeeding part, and the publisher's statement
giving his reasons for publishing the book.

State Library of N.S.W.: Mitchell Library; National Library.of
Australia.

Notes:
Part 2 has the date July 1859 and Gordon & Gotch has been added to
the list of publishers, Part 3 is dated August 1859, Part 4 is dated
September 1859. Part 4 concludes with the title page—on which
Binns & Goodwin, London & Bath, have joined the list of publish-
ers—the preface and the table of contents. Part I stops in mid-sen-

tence, two lines before the end of chapter xii. Part 2 finishes after Julie's poem near the end of chapter xxv. After that the publisher managed more skilfully. Part 3 finishes at the end of chapter xxxvi. Part 3 carries a notice saying that 'This work has a wide and increasing circulation in this and the adjoining colonies.'

The *Victorian Monthly Magazine* reviewed a second edition of Part 1 in July, 1869. Advertisements in *The South Australian Register* suggest that part 3 was soon out of print.

The Mortlock Library holds a copy of the parts bound in green leather with marbled covers and endpapers. The single word MARIAN, hand-finished in gold on a label of lighter green leather, has been pasted on the spine. The binder was J. Williams, Manufacturing Stationer, Adelaide. The stab marks for the binding can be clearly seen.

First English Edition 1860
MARIAN; or, The Light Of Some-One's Home. A Tale of Australian Bush Life.
BY MAUD JEAN FRANC. Bath: Binns & Goodwin. R.E. Peach. A. Waddy, Mount Barker, South Adelaide (sic). London: Darton & Co. n.d. [1860].
1 vol. 11.3 × 17 cm. pp. [iv] + vii + 407. Frontispiece. There is an added decorated title page opposite the frontispiece with a central circular illustration. Printer: Binns & Goodwin, Bath. No half title.

Pink rib-grained cloth over bevelled boards, stamped in blind on the front and back covers and blocked in gold on the front cover and spine. The covers have a blind decorated border with internal decorated corners which form an oval shape. In the centre of the front cover is a fine gold heart-shaped decoration with a spray of flowers rising from it. On the spine is the title MARIAN OR THE LIGHT OF SOME ONE'S HOME in gold, a spray of leaves below it and the publishers' names—Bath: Binns & Goodwin; London, Darton & Co.—at the bottom.

State Library of S.A.: Mortlock Library. This copy has been rebound but the original binding has been preserved.

Notes
This edition was published in October 1860 at 6s., and listed in the New Books Column of *The Publishers' Circular* on October 16. The

PART THREE – *Annotated Bibliography*

frontispiece and facing circular illustration were by Julian Portch, engraved by Edmund Evans. More than 800 copies were ordered by the London and export trade before the edition was ready for delivery. It was extensively advertised in *The Publishers' Circular* and was given a full page with the frontispiece as illustration in the Christmas number. The text does not differ significantly from the text of the Australian edition, alterations being mainly in punctuation.

The second English edition appeared in a heavy blue wavy-grain binding, undated, in June 1861. The type had been reset, the number of pages reduced to 377 and the words Second English Edition added to the title page. The name of R.E. Peach may or may not appear in the list of publishers. The price had been reduced from 6s. to 5s.

Anomalies in various copies of this edition suggest that demand for copies in the first half of 1861 was so strong that copies of the second edition were released early. According to *The Publishers' Circular* more than a thousand copies had been ordered before printing began.

The copy in the Mitchell library has the words Second English Edition and retains the name of the publisher R.E. Peach. A copy in the State Library of Victoria has 377 pages with the publisher Peach listed and the words Third Thousand on the title page but not Second English Edition. The Mortlock Library's copy has the words Second English Edition but no R.E. Peach. The blue binding of the copy in the State Library of Victoria appears to be sand-grain, not wavy-grain, but all three copies have the same fine gold device on the front and back covers.

The third edition appears in two forms. Each has the words Third Edition Revised on the title page. The first, published by Darton & Hodge, appeared undated, in December 1865 in green cloth over bevelled boards with gilt edges. There is a strong gold blocked circular design on the front cover with the words of the title standing out in relief. This edition retains the Portch frontispiece and illustrated title page. The frontispiece was used in a full page advertisement in the Christmas number of *The Publishers' Circular*.

At the beginning of 1866 Hodge and Darton parted company, Darton accusing Hodge of annexing their List of Religious Gift Books. Sampson Low, who had already acquired the right to publish Franc's next novel, *Vermont Vale*, which came out in April 1866, took over the copyright of *Marian*. Low published a second Third Edition of *Marian* in April 1867. Both Hodge and Low used the same printer, Butler and Tanner, but Low's edition has reset type and many changes had been made to punctuation. Low's edition is bound in dark green or brown sand grain cloth over bevelled boards, and is noted for the swash capitals which appear on the gold lettering on the spine. Portch's frontispiece is retained but there is no illustrated title page. All further editions and reissues of *Marian* were published by Low.

Fourth Edition 1868. pp. 377. Printer: Butler & Tanner. Frontispiece by G. P. Nicholls. This edition was also given a full page advertisement, including the frontispiece, in the Christmas number of *The Publishers' Circular*.

Fifth Edition 1873. pp. 376. Printer: Gilbert & Rivington. Frontispiece by Nicholls. The type was reset for the last time for this edition. Thereafter the type does not vary although a number of different printers and qualities of paper were used over the years. The following reissues have been sighted. I have not found copies of the seventh and eighth 'editions'.

Sixth Edition 1877. Ninth Edition 1883. Tenth Edition 1884. These are all in the Rose binding.

1888, 1889 and 1890 in the Daisy binding.

1894 in the Silver Floral binding.

1905 in the Leaf binding and in the Single Daisy binding.

1911 onwards (undated) in the Emu binding and Poppy binding.

1925 onwards (undated) in the Hockey and Lacrosse bindings and Plain Red binding.

This history of six separate editions and at least 20 subsequent reissues testifies to the popularity of this novel and of Franc as a novelist over a long period.

Reviews:
The Farm and Garden (Adelaide) 9 June, 8 July, 11 August 1859.
The Adelaide Observer 18 June 1859, repeated in *The South Australian Register* 20 June 1859.
Victorian Monthly Magazine July 1959.
The South Australian Register 18 July 1859.
The South Australian Advertiser 21 June 1859, repeated 18 July 1859, and in *The South Australian Weekly Chronicle* 25 June 1859
The Australian Evangelist (Melbourne) 31 August 1861.
The Athenaeum (London) 2 December 1865 under heading 'Children's Books.'

1866

VERMONT VALE; or Home Pictures in Australia.
BY MAUD JEANNE FRANC, Author of 'Marian; or, The Light of
Some One's Home'.
London: Sampson Low, Son, and Marston, Milton House, Ludgate
Hill. 1866. [The Right of Translation Reserved.]
1 vol. 11.5 × 17.7 cm. pp. viii + 329. Frontispiece. Printer: Harrild,
London. No half title.

Purple cloth over bevelled boards. There is a large central stylised
floral decoration and three lined borders stamped in blind on the
front and back covers. A stylised floral decoration is stamped in gold
on the spine with gold lettering of the full title near the top and the
publishers' imprint, SAMPSON LOW & Co , at the bottom. The
author's name does not appear on the covers or spine.
Library and Information Service of W. A.

Notes:
Vermont Vale appeared first as a serial in *The Australian Evangelist*
(Melbourne), where it ran from 15 August 1863 until 18 July 1864.

It was first published in London in April 1866, small post 8vo. at
5s. It was given a full page advertisement in *The Publishers' Circular* on
5 December 1866 with the frontispiece as illustration. The frontispiece of the country town Vermont Vale is by George French Angas.
It is not signed, but is attributed to Angas in the review in *The South
Australian Register*. The text does not differ significantly from the text
published in the *Evangelist*.

A second issue appeared on 1 March 1870 in the same binding as
the first. The cloth binding for this and the first issue appears in
several colours. The title page is the same except for the date, 1870,
but the printer is F. Bentley and Co., London. It has the Angas
frontispiece.

What was called the Third Edition appeared in the Rose binding
in 1876. A few slight differences suggest that the type had been reset,
and that this was in fact the second—and last—edition, although
there were many reissues with different dates on the title pages. The
printer was Gilbert and Rivington. It has the Angas frontispiece.

The Fourth Edition appeared in 1885, in the Rose binding, with
the same frontispiece and printer. *Vermont Vale* was reissued in the

cheap edition of 1888 in the Daisy binding, without the Angas frontispiece, and thereafter appeared in that binding and in others without dates. I have seen copies in Silver Floral, Leaf, Little Daisy, Poppy, Emu and Hockey bindings.

Reviews:
The Athenaeum (London) 9 June 1866.
The South Australian Advertiser 27 August 1866.
The Daily Telegraph (Adelaide) 27 August 1866.
Wallaroo Times 29 August and 8 September 1866.
The Kapunda Herald 31 August and 7 September 1866.
The Bunyip (Gawler) 1 September 1866.
The South Australian Register 17 September 1866.

1867

EMILY'S CHOICE: An Australian Tale.
BY MAUD JEANNE FRANC, Author of 'Marian', 'Vermont Vale', etc. London: Sampson Low, Son, and Marston. Milton House, Ludgate Hill. 1867. [The Right of Translation Reserved.]
    1 vol. 11.6 × 17.7 cm. pp. viii + 358 + 2 + 32. (Bound-in catalogue dated 1871.) Frontispiece. Printer: Bradbury, Evans, & Co., Whitefriars. No half title.

Red sand grain cloth cloth over bevelled boards, stamped in blind on the front and back covers and in gold on the spine. There are double ruled borders on the covers and a central large stylised floral decoration roughly oblong in shape. The spine is identical with the spine of the Rose binding. *Hall's Vineyard* appears in the same binding.
    State Library of N.S.W.: Mitchell Library.

Notes:
Emily's Choice first appeared as a serial in *The Australian Evangelist* (Melbourne) where it ran from 18 July 1865 to 18 June 1866 under the title *Joys and Sorrows*.
    It was first published in London in March 1867, small post 8vo. at 5s. The frontispiece of a man on horseback taking leave of a woman at the door of a cottage is by George French Angas—the initials G.F.A. can be seen at left—and was engraved by J. Cooper. Sampson Low's advertisements for the book give Angas's name as illustrator.

The text does not differ significantly from the text published in the *Evangelist*.

A copy in a binding similar to the binding of the copy in the Mitchell Library but dark blue in colour is in the possession of Mr John Congreve. It has an inscription to Emily Congreve 'from her sister the author.' It is dated 10 August 1867.

Emily's Choice was reissued in 1875 in the original binding and shortly after in the Rose binding and again in 1881 in the Rose binding, all with the Angas frontispiece. The words 'New Edition' are on the title pages, but it appears that all issues of *Emily's Choice* were printed from the original setting of type, however unlikely this seems. A misprint in the first line—'afavourable' instead of 'a favourable'—appeared first in 1881 and persisted until the Hockey binding era.

I have seen copies in the Daisy, Silver Floral, Leaf, Single Daisy, Emu, Poppy, Hockey and Lacrosse bindings.

Reviews:
The Athenaeum (London) 13 April 1867.
The Bunyip (Gawler) 17 August 1867.
The Express & Telegraph (Adelaide) 17 August 1867.
Wallaroo Times 21 August 1867.
The Kapunda Herald 30 August 1867.
Pasquin (Adelaide) 31 August 1867. *Emily's Choice* is not named but is discussed as the latest novel of the 'Vermont-Vale School.'

1869

GOLDEN GIFTS: An Australian Tale.
BY MAUD JEANNE FRANC, author of 'Marian', 'Vermont Vale', etc., etc. Kapunda: Scandrett & Elliott, Hill-Street. 1869. [All rights reserved.]
1 vol. 14 × 22.5 cm. pp. [vii] + 240. Printer: Scandrett & Elliott, Kapunda. No half title.

Purple irregularly grained cloth, with ruled borders and decorated corners stamped in blind on the front and back covers. The words GOLDEN GIFTS, A TALE, M.J. FRANC and a small triangular decoration are stamped in gold on the spine. The date is in gold at the bottom of the spine.

State Library of S.A.: Mortlock Library.

First English Edition 1883
GOLDEN GIFTS: An Australian Tale.
BY MAUD JEANNE FRANC, Author of 'Marian', 'Vermont Vale',
etc., etc. London, Sampson Low, Marston, Searle & Rivington,
Crown Buildings, 188, Fleet Street. 1883. [All rights reserved.]
1 vol. 11.6 × 17.7 cm. pp. [iv] + 316 + 32. (Bound-in catalogue dated
November 1882.) Printer: Gilbert & Rivington, Ltd. St John's
Square. No half title.
    Rose binding.
    State Library of S.A.: Mortlock Library

Notes:
Golden Gifts first appeared as a serial in *The Kapunda Herald* from 24
May 1867 to 6 March 1868. It appeared in book form in Australia in
October 1869 at 3s. 6d., having apparently been printed from the
type set for the newspaper. The columns used for the serial were a
different width from the rest of the paper.

A second edition, printed by Scandrett and Elliott from the original setting of type, was published in Adelaide by E. S. Wigg & Son in
September 1874 at 3s. Both these editions can be found in purple,
blue or green cloth binding, sometimes with and sometimes without
the date at the base of the spine. The text does not differ significantly
from that published in *The Kapunda Herald* although at least one paragraph has been omitted.

The first English edition was published in May 1883, small post
8vo. at 4s. This was the only one of Franc's novels not to receive
publication in London within a few years of publication in Australia,
possibly because of some special contract with the Australian publishers. It appeared later in the Daisy, Silver Floral, Leaf, Single Daisy
and Emu bindings. Apparently all English issues were printed from
the same settings of type. The text does not differ significantly from
the text of the Australian edition.

There is one problem copy. An Emu copy in the Australian
National Library is dated 1896, which is fifteen years too early for the
Emu binding. The printer is not one of those who usually printed for
the Emu binding but Gilbert and Rivington who were earlier printers.
The anomaly can be explained by the likelihood of unbound sheets
with a dated title page being still available when the reprinting which
took place for the Emu edition was undertaken.

Reviews:

I have been unable to find any reviews of *Golden Gifts* , a book suffi-ciently popular to receive a second Australian edition. This suggests that no review copies were sent.

1869

MINNIE'S MISSION. An Australian Temperance Tale.
BY MAUD JEAN FRANC. Printer's flower. London: Sampson Low, Son, & Marston, Crown Buildings, 188, Fleet Street. 1869.
1 vol. 11.6 × 17.7 cm. pp. vi + 296. Printer: Butler & Tanner, The Selwood Printing Works, Frome & London.

Purple cloth over bevelled boards, stamped in blind on the front and back covers and in gold on the spine. The covers have blind decora-tive borders at left and right, a ruled frame, and a small blind central circular motif, with decorative daggers at top and bottom. On the spine stamped in gold there is a stylised floral decoration of four small corner motifs, a larger central motif, and the publisher's imprint—LONDON, SAMPSON LOW & Co.—at the bottom. At the top a band stamped in gold allows the title and the words MAUD JEAN FRANC to stand out in relief.

Copy in my possession.

Notes:
Minnie's Mission appeared first as a serial in *The South Australian Temperance Herald*, published quarterly, where it ran from October 1866 until April 1870.

It was first published in London in May 1869, 12mo. at 4s., with a text that differs considerably from that published in the *Temperance Herald*. Minnie's surname had been changed from Royton to Rayton and many stylistic changes had been made. *Minnie's Mission* appeared in the Rose binding in 1876 and 1877 with the 1869 title page. For the Rose binding edition of 1878 the type had been reset and typographical errors corrected, although one significant error in paragraph five—'her brother's death' instead of 'his brother's death'—was not corrected, and persisted in all English issues. A Third Edition identical with the 1878 edition appeared in the Rose binding in 1885. The same setting of type was used for all subsequent reissues. I have seen copies in the Daisy, Silver Floral, Leaf, Single Daisy, Poppy, Emu and Hockey bindings.

Reviews:
The Kapunda Herald 15 October 1869.
The GawlerTimes and Goldfields Reporter 27 August 1869.
The Express and Telegraph (Adelaide) 14 October 1869. Repeated in
The South Australian Chronicle and Weekly Mail 16 October 1869.

1870

SILKEN CORDS AND IRON FETTERS. An Australian Tale.
BY MAUDE JEAN FRANC, Authoress of 'Marion', (*sic*) 'Vermont
Vale', 'Minnie's Mission', &c., &c. Gawler, S. A.: Whaley, Austin, &
Co., Printers and Publishers, The Gawler Times Office, Murray-
Street. 1870.
1 vol. 10.5 × 18 cm. pp. [v] + 219 + [9]. Printer: Whaley, Austin &
Co. No half title.

Green cloth with a wavy horizontal rib. There are plain borders
stamped in blind on the front and back covers with the title blocked
in gold on the front cover. SILKEN CORDS is curved and IRON
FETTERS straight. The spine is blank.
    State Library of S.A.: Mortlock Library.

First English Edition [1870]
SILKEN CORDS AND IRON FETTERS.
BY MAUDE JEAN FRANC. London: Sampson Low, Son & Marston,
Crown Buildings, 188, Fleet Street, E. C. n.d.
1 vol. 11.6 × 17.4 cm. pp. [vii] + 292 + 4. Printer: Butler & Tanner,
The Selwood Printing Works, Frome & London.

Green fine grain cloth over bevelled boards, stamped in blind on the
front and back covers and in gold on the spine. The covers have ruled
blind borders and a large central ruled oblong with four floriate circular decorations at the corners. Running down the spine in gold are
a small decoration, the title, the words MAUDE J. FRANC, a long
stylised decoration, and at the bottom the publisher's imprint, LON-
DON SAMPSON LOW & CO.
    State Library of S.A.: Mortlock Library.

Notes:
Silken Cords appeared first as a serial in *The Gawler Times and*

Goldfields Reporter where it ran from 5 November 1869 to 20 May 1870. It appeared in Australia in book form in green or other coloured cloth at 2s. 6d., before the end of 1870, the printers apparently using the type which had been set up for the serial, except for changes to accommodate decorative initial capitals, and a few alterations presumably made by the author.

The first English edition appeared in December 1870, small post 8vo. at 4s. It was reissued later in the Rose binding. Although the title pages do not carry dates bound-in catalogues for 1875 and 1881 give an indication of when this occurred. The fact that the publisher was still Sampson Low, Son & Marston shows that the original plates and title page were being used, for this publisher became Sampson Low, Marston, Low & Searle in 1871. The type was probably never reset, although a misprint was corrected for the 1888 Daisy edition. The text does not differ significantly from that of the Australian edition. I have also seen copies in the Silver Floral, Little Daisy, Leaf and Emu bindings.

Reviews:
Wallaroo Times 31 August 1870. Repeated in *The Bunyip* (Gawler) 10 September 1870.
The Evening Journal (Adelaide) 28 September 1870. Repeated in *The Adelaide Observer* 1 October 1870.
Truth and Progress (Adelaide) October 1870.
South Australian Bible Christian Magazine November 1870.
The Athenaeum (London) 3 December 1870 in 'Books for the Young.'

1874

JOHN'S WIFE.
BY MAUDE JEANNE FRANC, author of 'Marion', (*sic*) 'Minnie's Mission', etc., etc. London: Sampson Low, Marston, Low, & Searle. Crown Buildings, 188, Fleet Street. [All rights reserved.] n.d. 1 vol. 11.8 × 17.6 cm. pp. iv + 262 + 40. (Bound-in catalogue not dated.) Printer: Butler & Tanner, The Selwood Printing Works, Frome, and London.

Blue fine diagonally ribbed cloth over bevelled boards stamped in black on the front and back covers and in black and gold on the spine. The covers have a wide ruled decorated border adjacent to the spine and a central open oblong with two vertical and two horizontal decorated daggers. On the spine are the words JOHN'S WIFE and MAUDE JEANNE FRANC in fancy gold lettering near the top and the publisher's name—SAMPSON LOW—at the bottom. In between is a stylised floral design in black and gold with three flower buds at the top from the middle one of which extend three long gold stamens.

State Library of S.A.: Mortlock Library.

Notes:
John's Wife was published in May 1874, small post 8vo. at 4s. in green or blue cloth. Copies in the Rose binding have bound-in catalogues with dates 1876 and 1882. I have seen copies in the Daisy, Silver Floral, Poppy and Emu bindings. Apparently the same setting of type was used for all issues.

Reviews:
The Express and Telegraph (Adelaide)15 September 1874. Repeated in *The South Australian Chronicle and Weekly Mail* 19 September 1874.

1875

HALL'S VINEYARD.
BY MAUDE JEANNE FRANC, author of 'Marian', 'Vermont Vale', &c. &c. Publisher's Ornament. London: Sampson Low, Marston, Low, & Searle, Crown Buildings, 188, Fleet Street. [All rights reserved.] 1875.
1 vol. 11.5 × 17.7 cm. pp. [iv] + 266 + [2] + 40. (Bound-in catalogue dated October 1874.) Printer: Butler & Tanner, The Selwood Printing Works, Frome, and London. No half title.

Brown coloured cloth over bevelled boards, stamped in blind on the front and back covers and in gold on the spine. There are double ruled borders on the covers and a central large stylised floral decoration roughly oblong in shape. The spine is identical with the spine of the Rose binding. *Emily's Choice* appeared in the same binding.

State Library of S.A.: Mortlock Library.

Notes:
Hall's Vineyard was first published in London in March 1875, small post 8vo. at 4s., in brown or other coloured cloth, and was appearing in the Rose binding by 1876, though with the 1875 title page. I have seen copies in the Daisy, Silver Floral, Leaf and Emu bindings. Apparently the same setting of type was used for all issues.

Reviews:
The Express and Telegraph (Adelaide) 26 June 1875. Repeated in *The South Australian Chronicle and Weekly Mail* 3 July 1875.
The Adelaide Observer 10 July 1875.

1878

LITTLE MERCY; or, For Better, For Worse.
BY MAUDE JEANNE FRANC, Author of 'Marian', 'Vermont Vale', etc. etc. Printer's Ornament. London: Sampson Low, Marston, Searle, and Rivington, Crown Buildings, 188, Fleet Street. 1878. [All rights reserved.]
1 Vol. 11.5 × 17.7 cm. pp. vi + 303 + 24. (Bound-in catalogue dated September 1877.) Printer: John C. Wilkins and Vernon, 9 Castle Street, Chancery Lane.

Rose binding.
  State Library of S.A.: Mortlock Library.

Notes:
Little Mercy was first published on October 1877, small post 8vo. at 4s., although the title page date is 1878. It was reissued in 1879. The 1888 edition in the Daisy binding was a new edition, with the type reset and different decorations for chapter headings and endings. This edition was reissued as a 'Second Edition,' undated. (The copy I have seen has an inscription dated 30 August 1889 but it has been rebound.) A 'Third Edition' dated 1892 appeared in the Silver Floral binding, and a 'Fourth Edition,' undated, in the Leaf binding. These were the same as the Daisy edition but some misprints had been corrected. I have also noted a copy in the Emu binding.

Reviews:
The Academy (London) 15 December 1877. (Under heading 'Gift Books'.)

The Adelaide Observer 6 April 1878.
The South Australian Chronicle and Weekly Mail 8 June 1878. Repeated in *The Express and Telegraph* (Adelaide) 12 June 1878.

1880

BEATRICE MELTON'S DISCIPLINE.
BY MAUDE JEANNE FRANC, Author of 'Marian', 'Vermont Vale', 'Emily's Choice', 'John's Wife', 'Little Mercy', etc., etc. London; Sampson Low, Marston, Searle & Rivington, Crown Buildings, 188 Fleet Street. 1880. [All rights reserved.]
1 vol. 11.5 × 17.7 cm. pp. vii + 248 + 32. (Bound-in catalogue dated April 1880.) Printer: Gilbert & Rivington, St John's Square.

Rose binding.
    State Library of S.A.: Mortlock Library.

Notes:
Beatrice Melton's Discipline was first published in London in September 1880, small post 8vo at 4s. A 'Second Edition' appeared in the Rose binding in 1886. This is the only one of Franc's books which I have not seen in the 1888 Daisy binding issue which appeared shortly after her death. The fact that Sampson Low's *English Catalogue of Books* omits this book from its 1888 list suggests that it was not part of the Daisy edition. However in Low's advertisements for this first cheap edition *Beatrice Melton's Discipline* heads the list and I believe it is only a coincidence that I have not been able to find a copy. I have seen copies in the Leaf, Little Daisy, Emu and Hockey bindings. Apparently the same setting of type was used for all issues.

Reviews:
The Athenaeum (London) 27 November 1880. (Under the heading 'Christmas Books')
The Adelaide Observer 4 December 1880.
The Adelaide Observer 11 December 1880. (Under the heading 'Gossip about Children's Books')
The Express and Telegraph (Adelaide) 9 December 1880. Repeated in *The South Australian Chronicle and Weekly Mail* 18 December 1880.

1882

NO LONGER A CHILD.

BY MAUD JEAN FRANC, Author of 'Marian; or, the Light of Some One's Home', 'Vermont Vale', 'Little Mercy', etc., etc. London: Sampson Low, Marston, Searle & Rivington, Crown Buildings, 188, Fleet Street. 1882. [All rights reserved.]

1 vol. 11.5 × 17.7 cm. pp. vi + 311 + 32. (Bound-in catalogue dated December 1881.) Printer: Gilbert & Rivington, Limited, St John's Square.

Rose binding.
    State Library of S.A.: Mortlock Library.

Notes:
No Longer A Child , subtitled *A New Australian Story*, first appeared as a serial in *The Leader* (Melbourne) where it ran from 26 October 1878 until 8 February 1879.

    It appeared in London as a small post 8vo. at 4s. but I have found no record of the 1882 London publication date. The name Quinten as used in *The Leader* had been changed to Quinton but there are few other differences. A 'Second Edition' in the Rose binding was issued in 1885. I have seen copies in the Daisy, Silver Floral, Leaf, Poppy and Emu bindings. Apparently the same setting of type was used for all issues.

Reviews:
The South Australian Chronicle and Weekly Mail 21 October 1882.
The Adelaide Observer 21 October 1882.

1882

CHRISTMAS BELLS.

Edited by MAUDE JEANNE FRANC. Adelaide: Printed for Geo. Collis, Jun, Birks' Chambers, Rundle St., by J. H. Sherring & Co., 27, Currie St., 1882.

1 vol. 13.4 × 20.4 cm. pp. [2] + ii + 53. 5 full page illustrations by F. Burmeister. 4 pages of advertisements interleaved + 6 at back. No half title.

Thin greyish cardboard covers. The back cover and spine are blank. The front cover bears a coloured lithograph by J. H. Sherring & Co . A long spray of leaves and flowers almost encircles the title and editor's name. Towards the bottom there are illustrations of the spires of the General Post Office and the Adelaide Town Hall and of a river or lake with hills in the background. The printer's and publisher's names are at the bottom and the price—one shilling—at the top.

State Library of S.A.: Mortlock Library.

Notes:
This volume contains two stories by Franc: 'Unexpected: A Christmas Week's Experience', pp. 1-29, and 'In His Right Mind: A Tale of Christmas Eve', pp. 44-51. There are also two poems by Franc's son W[illiam] J[ames] Evans, and an anonymous story, 'Captain Peter Brown's Christmas', which was almost certainly by Franc's older son, Henry Congreve Evans. The irreverent jocular style is consistent with his other published work.

I have found no reviews of this little book.

1883

'TWO SIDES TO EVERY QUESTION', From a South Australian Standpoint.
BY MAUDE JEANNE FRANC, author of 'Marian', 'Emily's Choice', 'John's Wife', etc., etc. London: Sampson Low, Marston, Searle, & Rivington, Crown Buildings, 188, Fleet Street. 1883. [All rights reserved.]
1 vol. 11.5 × 17.7 cm. pp. vii + 229 + [1] + 32. (Bound-in catalogue dated November, 1882.) Printer: Gilbert and Rivington, Ltd, St John's Square.

Rose binding.
State Library of S.A.: Mortlock Library.

Notes:
Two Sides to Every Question appeared first as a serial in *The Illustrated Adelaide News* where it ran from January 1876 until February 1877.

It was first published in London in March 1883, post 8vo. at 4s., with a text which did not differ significantly from the text published in the *News*. I have seen copies in the Daisy, Silver Floral, Leaf, Poppy and Emu bindings. Apparently all issues were printed from the same setting of type.

Reviews:
The Adelaide Observer 2 June 1883.
The South Australian Chronicle and Weekly Mail 2 June 1883.

1885

INTO THE LIGHT.

BY MAUD JEAN FRANC, Author of 'Marian', 'Minnie's Mission', and other stories. London: Sampson Low, Marston, Searle, & Rivington, Crown Buildings, 188, Fleet Street. 1885. [All rights reserved.]
1 vol. 11.5 × 17.7 cm. pp. viii + 272 + [2]. Printer: Gilbert & Rivington, Limited, St John's Square.

Rose binding.
    State Library of S.A.: Mortlock Library.

Notes:
Into the Light first appeared as a serial in two parts in *The Christian Colonist* (Adelaide). The first part, 'Into the Light', ran from 15 October 1880 until 11 February 1881, and the second, 'Walking in the Light', from 11 January 1884 until 11 April 1884.
    It was first published in London in April 1885, small post 8vo. at 4s. with a text which did not differ significantly from the text published in the *Colonist*. I have seen copies in the Daisy, Silver Floral, Leaf and Emu bindings. Apparently all issues were printed from the same setting of type.

Reviews:
The Adelaide Observer 23 May 1885.
The Bunyip (Gawler) 29 May 1885.
The South Australian Chronicle and Weekly Mail 6 June 1885.

1885

THE MASTER OF RALSTON.

BY MAUD JEANNE FRANC, Author of 'Marian', 'No Longer a Child', 'Two Sides to Every Question', 'John's Wife', 'Golden Gifts', 'Into the Light', etc., etc.

> 'Gold! gold! gold! gold
> Bright and yellow, hard and cold.

> 'How widely its agencies vary,
> To save, to ruin, to curse, to bless.'
> Hood.

London: Sampson Low, Marston, Searle, & Rivington, Crown Buildings, 188, Fleet Street. 1885. [All rights reserved.]
1 vol. 11.5 × 17.7 cm. pp. iv + 300 + [2] + 32. (Bound-in catalogue dated October 1885.) Printer: Gilbert & Rivington, Ltd. St. John's Square. No half title.

Rose binding.
    State Library of S.A.: Mortlock Library.

Notes:
The Master of Ralston was first published in London in December 1885, small post 8vo. at 4s. I have seen copies in the Daisy, Silver Floral, Leaf, Emu and Hockey bindings. In the Emu binding issues the name Ralston is spelt Railston on the cover and spine, although it is correct on the title page and throughout the novel. Apparently all issues were printed from the same setting of type.

Reviews:
The Adelaide Observer 13 February 1886.
The Bunyip (Gawler) 19 February 1886.
The South Australian Chronicle and Weekly Mail 27 February 1886.

Other Writings

In *The Australian Evangelist*

1861 18 July   'Little Willie or the early called.' by Maud Jean Franc. [A story for children in four chapters.]

1862 18 February   'Jessie's adventure, or lost and found.' by Maud Jean Franc. [A story for children and a poem.]

3 April   'Weep not.' by Maud Jeanne Franc. [A devotional piece.]

3 June   'The old Dingle farm.' by Maud Jeanne Franc. [A story.]

18 October   'Speak the truth.' by Maud Jeanne Franc. [A story for children.]
'The starless Crown.' by Maud Jeanne Franc. [A poem.]

1863 21 March   'Ebby's Hen.' by Maud Jeanne Franc. [A story for children in three chapters.]

21 March   'The "forgotten resting place".' by Maud Jeanne Franc. [A story in five chapters and two parts.] Concluded on June 3.

3 June   'Little Charlie.' by Maud Jeanne Franc. [A poem.]

1864 18 March   'Miss Mary Ellen Wansbrough.' by M.J.E. [An obituary.]

1865 18 February   'The one jewel.' by Maude Jeanne Franc.
'The gentle boy.'
'Isn't it almost time?'
'The pet-dog that had one fault.'
'A word from a child.'
[Five short stories for children.]
'The three roses.' by Maude Jeanne Franc. [A poem.]

18 March   'The mansion prepared.' by Maude Jeanne Franc. [A poem.]
'Prayer-bells.' by Maude Jeanne Franc. [A story.]

In *The South Australian Temperance Herald*
1872   August   *Jem's hopes; and what they grew to.* by Maude
                        Jean Franc. [A serial in more than four chapters
                        and four parts.] Monthly until November.
                        [Conclusion unknown: following issues missing.]

In *Truth and Progress*
1870   April   'Trust.' by M.J.E. [A devotional piece.]
1871   October   'A father's hand.' by M.J.E. [A devotional piece.]
1875   Septemb.   'Divine guidance.' by M.J.E. [A poem.]
1881   1 April   'Jesus knows.' by M.J.E. [A poem.]
1884   1 July   'A crook in the lot.' by Maud Jeanne Franc.
                        [A story.]

In *South Australian Christmas Annual*
1881   'Ellie Venn, and what Christmas brought to her.'
                        by Maude Jeanne Franc. [A story in two parts.]

In *The Christian Colonist*
1882 14 April   'The burdens of life and how to bear them.' by
                        Maud Jeanne Franc. [A serial in three chapters
                        and three parts.] Weekly until April 28.
1885 3 July   *Wooden crosses.* by Maude Jean Franc. [A serial
                        in nine chapters and thirteen parts.] Weekly until
                        September 25. [Last issue missing.]

In *The South Australian Chronicle and Weekly Mail*
1882 23 December   'Tom Morison's golden Christmas.' by Maude
                        Jeanne Franc. [A story in six chapters.]
1883 22 December   'By our own door: a Christmas gift.' by Maude
                        Jeanne Franc. [A story in six chapters.]
1884 20 December   'The Child Bella and Her Happy Christmas.' by
                        Maude Jeanne Franc. [A story in four chapters.]
                        'How Annie saved me: a Christmas day's
                        adventure.' by Maude Jeanne Franc.
                        [A story in six chapters.]
1885 19 December   'Underneath: a Christmas day's revelations.' by
                        Maude Jeanne Franc. [A story in seven chapters.]
1886 25 December   'Dr. Harden's theories: a Christmas climax.' by
                        the late Maud Jeanne Franc.
                        [A story in seven chapters.]

Thomas Gill's *Bibliography of South Australia* (1886) lists, besides the works I have listed, three stories published by F.W.Robinson in the Crystal Stories Series (London).

> *Fern Hollow*
> *Jem's Hopes*
> *At the Well*

I have not been able to find out anything about this series.

I have found no other record of *Fern Hollow*, but a novel *Fern's Hollow* by Sara Smith ('Hesba Stretton') was published in London in 1864 by the Religious Tract Society. *Jem's Hopes* (1872) published in Adelaide in the *S.A Temperance Herald*, and presumably after that in the Crystal Series, clearly shows the influence of Smith's work. It is possible that Gill was mistaken and that *Fern Hollow* referred to Smith's work. I have found no other record of *At The Well*.

Gill lists also *Out of the Wine Vat* which he says was published in the *Temperance Herald*, Melbourne. I have not been able to locate either the publication or the story .

Henry John Congreve

Maud Jeanne Franc's brother, Henry John Congreve, was also a writer in a small way. His essays on mining and sketches of pioneering days are worth preserving, although he was less successful as a short story writer. He contributed to *The History of the Inglewood Reefs from their Discovery in 1859 to 1866* by Thomas Howard, originally written for *The Inglewood Sentinel*, later *The Inglewood Advertiser*. He also contributed additions and a summary to the second edition printed and published by *The Inglewood Advertiser* in 1883. These articles are not the same as those listed below on the same subject and published in 1864, though they deal with many of the same mining areas. He also published in a number of newpapers using the pseudonyms Honricus and H.J.C.

I have listed below in chronological order those writings which I have located. The papers involved are *The Inglewood Advertiser*, *The Australasian*, *The Adelaide Observer*, *The South Australian Chronicle and Weekly Mail*, *The Gawler Standard*, and *The Bunyip* (Gawler). I expect that there are still others to be found, especially in Victorian newspapers.

1864	29 October	*A History of the Inglewood Reefs* Chapter I	*Inglewood* *Advertiser*
	1 November	Chapter II	
	3 November	Chapter III	
	5 November	Chapter IV	
	8 November	Chapter V	
	19 November	Chapter VI	
	22 November	A Letter from Honricus: 'Health and how to keep it.'	
	24 November	*A History of the Reefs*. Chapter VII A Letter from Honricus: 'Health—Water.'	
	26 November	A Letter from Honricus: 'Health—Clothing.'	

	1 December	*A History of the Reefs.* Chapter VIII	*Inglewood*
	10 December	Chapter IX	*Advertiser*
	15 December	Chapter X	
	22 December	Chapter XI	
	24 December	'Christmases I Have Spent' by Honricus	
	29 December	*A History of the Reefs.* Chapter XII	
1868	16 May	'An Adventure in the Scrub in '49.' by Honricus	*Australasian*
1880	13 November	'Death of a Bush Hermit.'	*Observer*
	25 December	'The Ghostly Digger.'	*Observer*
	25 December	'Winning a Wife: A Bush Yarn.'	*Chronicle*
	25 December	'A Puddler's Christmas Yarn.'	*Standard*
1881	1 January	'The Siege of Limestone Well Camp.'	*Observer*
	8 January	'Nuggetty Sandy.'	*Observer*
	22 January	'Driven from Digging: A Victorian Episode.'	*Observer*
	5 February	'Wild Dog Adventures.'	*Observer*
	19 February	'How He Left and Where He Found Her: A Diggings Tragedy.'	*Observer*
	26 February	'My Dog Jessie.'	*Observer*
	12 March	'Prospecting for Gold.'	*Observer*
	2 April	'His Wife's Dream: A Story of the Victorian Diggings.'	*Observer*
	14 May	'A Legend of Spillsby Island.'	*Observer*
	28 May	'Loved to the Last: An Old Bush Yarn.'	*Observer*
	16 July	'The Rose of Mickleford.'	*Observer*
	30 July	'The Death Light: A Legend of Possum Gully.'	*Observer*
	20 August	'Too Late: or Jack the Dreamer.'	*Observer*
	24 September	'The Adventures of Billy Button.'	*Observer*
	19 November	'Nunilqie.'	*Observer*
	10 December	'Jimmy the Ringer.'	*Observer*
	24 December	'Gold and Danger or A Digger's Christmas.'	*Standard*
1882	14 January	'Brave Nellie.'	*Observer*
	1 July	'A Mysterious Voice: A Legend of the Barossa.'	*Observer*

	29 July	' "Old Scottie," the Ishmaelite.'	*Observer*
	21 October	'Stoitt's Pass: or Meeting a Madman.'	*Observer*
	23 December	'The Christmas Reef: or The Fortunes of Tom and Sandy.'	*Observer*
1883	25 June	'Was it Illusion?'	*Observer*
	14 July	'Scarlet Jim.'	*Observer*
	20 October	'Silky Richard.'	*Observer*
	20 December	'A Strange Career.'	*Observer*
1884	24 May	'Jim Dogan.'	*Observer*
	23 August	'Saved by an Eclipse.'	*Observer*
1885	13 March – 22 May	*Old Roach' and His Adopted Daughter.*	*Bunyip*
	5 June – 17 July	*'Nulingee': an Australian Tale of Bush and Diggings.*	*Bunyip*
	24 July – 11 Dec.	*Change and Mystery.*	*Bunyip*
	24 December (Supp)	'Mochtz or How Teetulpa saved them.'	*Bunyip*
1886	15 January	'Nan, the Dance Girl.'	*Bunyip*
	22 January	'Silky Richard.'	*Bunyip*
	25 December	'Nell: or Grampian Mysteries.'	*Observer*
1887	13 May – 28 Oct.	*Gordon Balderstone or The Unfulfilled Prediction.*	*Bunyip*
	11 Nov. – 18 Nov.	'Jim Dogan, the Old Soldier.'	*Bunyip*
	23 December (Supp)	'Jessica and Glendulph: or Love's Trials: A Tale of Ancient Gawler.'	*Bunyip*
1888	20 April – 19 Oct	*'Clarise' or Which is the Man?*	*Bunyip*
1889	4 January	'The Rolling Cloud: or Ralph Tremaine's New Year Gift.'	*Bunyip*
1890	3 January	'Red Ruff or A New Year's Deliverance.'	*Bunyip*

Notes and Sources

Where possible sources have been identified in the text. Some sources in constant use are listed here. Others are listed under the relevant chapters.

Much information about the life of Matilda Evans has been gained from obituaries and newspaper comments published between 23 and 30 October 1866 in *The Bunyip* (Gawler), *The South Australian Chronicle and Weekly Mail*, *The Express and Telegraph*, *The Kapunda Herald*, *The South Australian Register* and *The Christian Colonist*, and from papers relating to the Congreve family in the possession of Mr John Congreve of Sydney. Obituaries of Henry John Congreve in *The Bunyip* (19 July 1918) and *The Observer* (20 July 1918) have been useful as well as his reminiscences published in *The Register* 31 March 1909. There are also obituaries of Emily (*The Chronicle* and *The Observer*, 3 October 1896), Frederick (*The Chronicle* and *The Observer*, 22 September 1906) and William Congreve (*The Chronicle* and *The Observer*, 27 July 1907). Obituaries of Matilda's sons also contain information: Henry Evans in *Quiz*, 12 January 1899, *The Kapunda Herald*, 13 January, *The Critic*, *The Chronicle* and *The Observer*, 14 January, and in *The Northern Argus*, 20 January; William Evans in *The Chronicle* and *The Observer*, 24 September 1904, *The Critic*, 28 September and *Quiz*, 30 September. Obituaries of the Reverend John Baptist Austin in *The Chronicle*, 2 April 1882, and his son John Baptist Austin in *The Observer*, 9 September 1896, were consulted.

Matilda's teaching career as well as the careers of her husband, sister and brothers have been reconstructed from the minutes of the Central Board of Education, from newspaper reports of the meetings of the Board and from the Education Reports in the S.A. Government Gazettes.

Rate assessment records in the City of Adelaide Archives and in the Angaston Council Archives provided information about houses, their nature, size, value and occupants. There are no early records for Mount Barker.

Much information about the publication of Matilda's novels is to be found in *The Publishers' Circular*, published by Sampson Low and available at Melbourne and Sydney Universities on microfiche. Some information about Matilda's life as well as about her novels is to be found in the reviews, all of which are listed in the Annotated Bibliography.

Books which have been of special assistance have been mentioned in the text or in the chapter sources, but Paul Depasquale's *A Critical History of South Australian Literature* must be singled out. It is an invaluable reference tool.

To familiarise myself with the period I read or consulted dozens of books newspapers and periodicals. Of particular value were Douglas Pike's *Paradise of Dissent*, *The Flinders History of South Australia* edited by Dean Jaensch and Eric Richards, *Learning and Other Things: Sources for a Social History of Education* in South Australia, edited by B. Hyams et al., Alison Mackinnon's *One Foot on the Ladder*, Helen Jones' *In Her Own Name*, Paula Nagel's *North Adelaide 1837-1901*, and the Kensington and Norwood Council's Fify Years' *History of the Town of Kensington and Norwood*.

For the bibliography I gained particular help from the many publications of F. T. Bowers, Philip Gaskell, G. T. Tanselle, Michael Sadleir, John Carter, Ruari McLean and Douglas Ball.

Throughout this undertaking I have been constantly encouraged by Carolyn Heilbrun's *Writing a Woman's Life*.

CHAPTER SOURCES

Chapter 1

The Congreve papers contain extracts from a British Baptist publication *The Earthen Vessel*. The issue for August-September 1853 has an article by Matilda's half-brother George Thomas Congreve which deals with the life and death of their father. An earlier article, in March 1853, is a memoir by George of his stepmother, Elizabeth. Henry's and George's publications are listed in the British Museum's *Catalogue of Printed Books*. Shipping lists for the *Trafalgar* and *Chatham* give information about the voyages as does *The Adelaide Morning Chronicle*, 5 July 1852.

Chapter 2

The inquest on Henry Congreve was reported in *The Adelaide Morning Chronicle* on 20 December 1852 and in *The Register* on 21 December.

Chapter 3

Obituaries of Walter Paterson in *The Mount Barker Courier* (4 May 1894) and *The Chronicle* (5 May 1894) give much information about him and the district. *The Aldine History of South Australia* by W. Frederic Morrison contributed to my knowledge of Walter Paterson and of the period in general. The Pew Book of the Mount Barker Presbyterian Church is in the Mortlock Library.

Chapter 4

Information about the price and marketing of Spence's novels comes from *The Publishers' Circular*. On 22 February 1864 *The Telegraph* carried an advertisement announcing the forthcoming publication of *Uphill Work* in *The Weekly Mail*. Unfortunately there are no existing copies of *The Weekly Mail*.

Chapter 5

The recent biography of Darwin by Adrian Desmond and James Moore deals with the impact of Darwin's unbelief on his marriage

Chapter 6

Much of the information about Ephraim Evans's life comes from an obituary in *The Australian Evangelist*, 3 June 1863. His arrival in the *Leonidas* is recorded in *The Adelaide Times*, 5 December 1853. The death certificate of his first child shows where they lived in Adelaide. The circumstances of Evans's death are recorded in the Lyndoch report in *The Register*, 10 April 1863, and in a report of the opening of the South Rhine Baptist Chapel in *The Register*, 15 April 1863.

Other sources are the Lyndoch Baptist Church Centenary pamphlet and the Lyndoch Valley Baptist Church Minute Book, the Baptist Church records of Zion Chapel, Salt Creek, all in the Mortlock Library, and the history of the Baptist Church in South Australia by H. Estcourt Hughes, *Our First Hundred Years*. (Hughes's account of the opening of the South Rhine Chapel conflicts with newspaper accounts.) Reg Butler's monumental history of the Mount Pleasant district, *The Quiet Waters By*, also gives information about

Evans's connection with the churches and schools in the district. It is a mine of information about the times.

The district of the South Rhine, so often referred to in contemporary accounts, cannot be found on modern maps. The Hundred of South Rhine became the Hundred of Jutland in 1918, and the South Rhine River was renamed the River Marne. In spite of this the river is still called the South Rhine or Rhine by local people, and the expression South Rhine is still used.

Chapter 7

Some of the information about schools in Angaston comes from *The Barossa: A Vision Realised: The Nineteenth Century Story* edited by Reginald S. Munchenberg. This book gives good background material. The obituary for Mary Ellen Wansbrough appeared in *The Australian Evangelist* 18 March 1864. Amazingly the Angaston Baptist Church Sunday School Attendance booklets for 1865 have survived and are in the Mortlock Library.

There are many accounts of the wine industry in the area and of the Angas family. I particularly consulted *Keyneton 1839-1980* by Geoffrey B. Saegenschnitter. An article by George Bell, 'South Australian Wine and the London Market 1858-1876' in the *Journal of the Historical Society of South Australia*, no. 20, 1992, gives information about the adulteration of wine. The alcoholic content of wine was frequently discussed in newspapers at the time. Trollope's comments are to be found in his *Australia*.

The report of John Howard Angas's address at the meeting to consider establishing an Inebriate Asylum is in *The Register*, 19 February 1874. Some part of the later history of Pollie and Ebenezer Evans is to be found in *Between the Lines*, the history of the Lines family edited by Heather Brown. Sue and Newton Lines of Tarlee also supplied me with information from family papers. Henry John Congreve's marriage certificate, now in the possession of John Congreve, gave details about his wedding. William Congreve was a witness.

Chapter 8

Angaston-Cottage was advertised in both *The South Australian Advertiser* and *The Register* from 6 to 17 March 1869. Advertisements giving the dates for the return of pupils after vacation appeared regularly each quarter in both papers and sometimes gave information about vacancies, charges or movement to new premises. Matilda's letters are in the possession of John Congreve. Useful 'Town Tattle' columns by 'Cit' appeared in *The Bunyip* on 13 January 1899 and 30 September 1904.

Chapter 9
The minute book for the meetings of the deaconesses of the North Adelaide Baptist Church is in the Mortlock Library. The report of Rev. W. Rice's sermon appeared in *The Register* 1 November 1886.

Chapter 10
Margaret Allen's thesis, *Three South Australian Women Writers, 1854-1923*, (Flinders University) contributed much to my understanding of the social aspects of Matilda's work.

Chapter 14
Any reader who wishes for more information about the terms 'implied author,' 'implied reader,' 'narrator' and 'narratee' should consult *Narrative Fiction: Contemporary Poetics* by Shlomith Rimmon-Kenan (1983). I discussed the matter at some length in my book *The Narrator's Voice: The Dilemma of Children's Fiction* (1991).

ILLUSTRATIONS

I am grateful to the Mortlock Library for permission to print photographs of bindings, dustjackets and frontispieces of some of Maud Jeanne Franc's novels, reference number SSL: M: Z829.3 F814

Index

WAKEFIELD PRESS

MAISIE

HER LIFE IN HER LETTERS FROM 1898 TO 1902
edited by Joan Kyffin Willington

In 1898 Maisie Smith is twenty and on board ship from London to her South Australian birthplace to recover from a 'disastrous engagement'. By the time she arrives she has won and broken new hearts and is fresh for adventures in Adelaide, Sydney, Melbourne and the bush.

ISBN 1 86254 282 1 (hard)   RRP $39.95
ISBN 1 86254 320 8 (paper)   RRP $19.95

SOMEONE YOU KNOW

A FRIEND'S FAREWELL
Maria Pallotta-Chiarolli

Someone You Know is Maria Pallotta-Chiarolli's biography of Jon, who is living with AIDS, and the story of their extraordinary friendship. The threads and entanglements of their lives come together at Jon's final gathering.

ISBN 1 86254 271 6   RRP $14.95

WAKEFIELD PRESS

Wakefield Press has been publishing good Australian books for over fifty years. For a catalogue of current titles, or to add your name to our mailing list, send your name and address to Wakefield Press, Box 2266, Kent Town South Australia 5071.

TELEPHONE (08) 362 8800   FAX (08) 362 7592